THE POST-WAR WORLD

THE USSR SINCE 1945

ELIZABETH CAMPLING

B.T. Batsford Ltd, London

CONTENTS

First published 1990

Typeset by Tek-Art Ltd, Kent and printed in Great Britain by The Bath Press, Bath for the publishers B.T. Batsford Ltd 4 Fitzhardinge Street London W1H 0AH

ISBN 0 7134 6063 6

Acknowledgments
The Author and Publishers would like to thank the following for permission to reproduce illustrations: Camera Press for pages 29 and 40 (*top*); The Hulton Picture Company for pages 7 (*right*) and 19; Novosti Press Agency for pages 4, 7 (*bottom*), 40 (*top*), 54 (*bottom*) and 55 (*bottom*) and 55 (*bottom*); Topham Picture Library for pages 8, 12 (*top and bottom*), 20, 24, 28, 31, 33, 34, 36, 38 (*top and bottom*), 42, 44, 45, 46, 47, 49, 50, 54 (*top*) and 57. The maps on pages 4 and 15 were drawn by Robert Brien.

Cover illustrations (*Top*) Raisa and Mikhail Gorbachev (courtesy Rex Teatures); (*left*) Joseph Stalin (courtesy The Hulton Picture Company); (*centre*) Workers accommodation at the Serp i Molot steel plant (courtesy Novosti Press Agency); (*left*) the Soviet Space Shuttle (courtesy Novosti Press Agency).

The frontispiece shows Ronald Reagan introducing Mikhail Gorbachev to President elect George Bush, December 1988 (courtesy Topham Picture Company).

1 THE ROAD TO 1945

It is incorrect to use the term 'Russia' or 'Russians' to describe the state or its inhabitants, as the Russians are only one of a number of ethnic groups that make up the USSR. However, as these terms are so often used by the Western media, it is sometimes impossible to avoid them altogether.

In 1945 the territory of the Union of Soviet Socialist Republics covered one sixth of the world's land surface, making it the world's largest nation. It spread across 11 time zones and almost as many climatic ones, from the tundra of the Arctic Circle to the deserts of Central Asia. The population of around 170 million was made up of 24 different nationalities, each with its own distinctive history, language and culture, of whom the most numerous were the Russians, who lived in the region known as European Russia between the Polish frontier and the Ural Mountains. In 1945 this vast multinational state was at the end of 30 of the most momentous and stormy years of its history.

The Marxist State

In November 1917, in the midst of the First World War, the Communists, under Lenin, had seized power in Russia and have held on to it ever since. The country they took over was economically backward, with primitive agriculture and widespread illiteracy. Its industries lagged far behind those of Western Europe.

Followers of the ideas of Karl Marx (1818-1883), as set down in *The Communist Manifesto* (1848) and *Das Kapital* (1867).

The Communists were Marxists, for whom the main driving force of history was the conflict between social classes, arising from economic development. The climax of this development would occur under capitalism, when the exploited working class or proletariat would rise up in rebellion against the unjust capitalist system and replace it with socialism, the perfect society. Class conflict would disappear, the benefits of modern technology be available to all and men live and work co-operatively together in a true socialist democracy. In time, the state itself, unnecessary in such a Utopia, would wither away. Historically, the triumph of Socialism was inevitable and would happen everywhere, although at different speeds. In time, there would be no frontiers and no wars, just universal brotherhood.

In Marxist philosophy, the USA and the states of Western Europe are capitalist states.

To describe how the socialist society would work, Marx coined the famous phrase 'from each according to his ability, to each according to his need'.

From the beginning Russia did not fit the Communist ideal. It was a country of peasants with few industrial workers. The Communists had many enemies and the revolution did not spread, as they had hoped, into Germany or Western Europe. Before long the vision of socialist democracy had given way to a dictatorship of the Communist Party itself, whose job it was to protect the new state against its enemies, inside and out, and to raise the consciousness of the masses until they were ready to run things for themselves. Soviet Russia was not yet a socialist state but a temporary Dictatorship of the Proletariat, under the guidance of the Communist Party of the Soviet Union or CPSU. No other political parties were permitted and opposition suppressed by the Cheka or secret police. A large class of professional party administrators grew up. They were known as *apparachiks* and formed the élite of the new nation.

Party members were supposed to do their job out of a sense of mission and not for personal gain. Early leaders like Lenin lived simply and gave themselves only modest salaries. In time, however, party membership brought more and more privileges and formed a kind of Communist upper class.

Lenin – the father of the Soviet State.

Secede: to withdraw from a nation.

With the annexation of the Baltic States (Latvia, Lithuania, Estonia) and Moldavia in 1940, the number of socialist republics was raised to 15 and has stayed the same since.

The voting age is now 18.

Between 1918 and 1946 ministers were called commissars and the Council of Ministers, the Council of Commissars.

The USSR, the largest country in the world.

In other ways, the Communist government did all it could to make a clean break with the past and create a new kind of society. Women were given full equality and encouraged to play an active role in economic and political life. Divorce and abortion were made easy. Religion, which Marx had dubbed the 'opium of the people', was discouraged and often persecuted, although not forbidden outright. Atheism became the official creed of the state. Health care and education were free and open to all. Prices for the necessities of life like rent, fares on public transport and basic foods were kept deliberately low, a custom that has continued to the present day.

The Soviet Constitution

In 1922 the country was renamed the Union of Soviet Socialist Republics (USSR) or Soviet Union and in 1936 given a new constitution, which was still in force in 1945. On paper the USSR was a federal and democratic state. There were 11 socialist republics, each with wide powers over its own internal affairs and the right to secede, if they wanted to. Throughout the country each area was governed by a local *soviet* or council, elected by everyone over the age of 21. In turn, the soviets chose representatives to the Supreme Soviet, which met in Moscow, the capital, and chose the Council of Ministers or Praesidium, the nation's official government. It was headed by the Chairman of the Council of Ministers, or Prime Minister, and the President.

Much of the democracy and federalism was a sham, however. Only party members could stand for election to the soviets and there was usually only one candidate, putting the government firmly in the hands of the CPSU. The Supreme Soviet, which only met for a few days each autumn, did little more than rubber-stamp decisions made by the party bosses. Party-control in the individual republics kept them loyal to Moscow and made nonsense of their

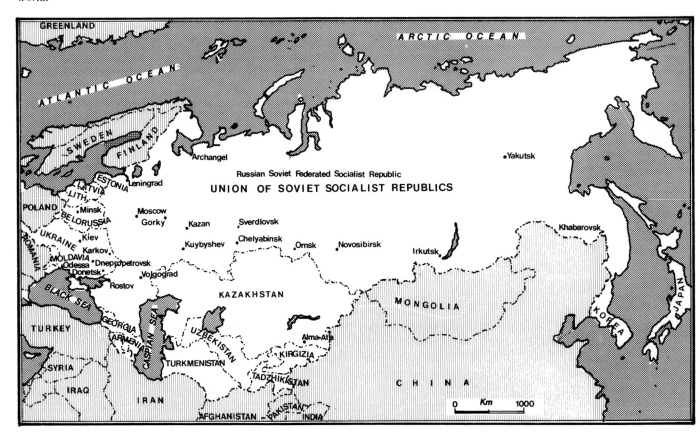

federal rights. And there was little democracy in the party itself, for officials were sent out from Moscow rather than chosen by the local membership. Real power in the USSR rested, therefore, with the handful of top Communists who made up the party Politburo and controlled all the vital appointments.

The Stalinist State

After Lenin's death in 1924, rivalry among his successors brought Joseph Stalin to the top. As General Secretary of the CPSU in charge of appointments, Stalin had planted his supporters in key positions throughout the Party and was able to out-vote and out-manoeuvre his main rival, Leon Trotsky, at every turn. By 1929 he had made the post of Secretary the most important in the Party and himself the most powerful man in the Soviet Union.

From the end of 1934, Stalin began to purge the party of any potential rivals. Leading communists like Kamenev and Zinoviev were forced to confess to unlikely crimes, given a brief trial and shot. Soon the Terror spread to include anyone, great or small, whose loyalty to the Soviet system was even the slightest bit in doubt. Over the next few years, millions died or disappeared into the labour camps of Siberia and the Arctic Circle, from which few ever returned. The party was decimated, so too was the officer corps of the Red Army. Those appointed to fill the vacancies owed their careers and their lives to Stalin or had been cowed into obedience. Party dictatorship had been replaced by one-man dictatorship. The Soviet Union became a country of fear, memories of which etched themselves deep into the national consciousness. The secret police, now renamed the NVKD, who ran the labour camps, were given sweeping powers. Its chief was second in power only to Stalin himself.

Stalin used his great power to bring all Soviet life under his control. All art, culture and education was forced into the service of the state, and those who could not conform were silenced. History was rewritten to suit Stalin. The NVKD encouraged neighbours to spy on one another, so that few people knew whom they could trust. Stalin himself had become the subject of a cult, which taught that he could do no wrong. By 1939 few Russians born after 1920 would ever have come across an opinion questioning the official line that Stalin was all-wise and Soviet society superior in all respects to capitalist ones. The Soviet Union had became a totalitarian state.

The Modernization of the USSR

Between 1928 and 1940 the USSR was industrialized. It was done by creating what became known as a command economy. Gosplan, the state planning agency, drew up a series of Five-Year Plans, which set targets for each industry, allocated resources, set prices and directed labour where it was needed. Workers were forbidden to leave their jobs without permission, and absenteeism was severely punished. To train a skilled labour force, free, nationwide primary education was established and illiteracy all but wiped out. The cost to the Soviet people was great, but by allowing the state to concentrate resources where they wanted to, by 1940 the USSR was on its way to becoming an urbanized nation and an industrial giant. Without the Five-Year Plans the country might not have survived the German invasion of 1941. The following figures give some idea of the speed of the transformation.

Leon Trotsky (1879-1940) had been Lenin's right-hand man during the 1917 revolution and founded the Red Army. He was exiled from the USSR in 1929 and assassinated in Mexico in 1940 by a Stalinist agent. Lev Kamenev (1883-1936) and Grigory Zinoviev (1883-1936) had also been close colleagues of Lenin in 1917.

The trials were called 'show trials' because their purpose was to display to the world the guilt of the accused, which had already been decided on.

The camps were known as the *Gulag* after the Russian initials for the Commissariat of Internal Affairs, which administered them. The author, Alexander Solzhenitzyn, who was in one from 1945, has written a three-part history, based on interviews with hundreds of survivors, entitled *The Gulag Archipelago* (Fontana, 1978).

All artistic works had to conform to the style known as Socialist Realism, which idealized the struggle of the Soviet people in building up their country and blamed all the problems on 'class enemies' and traitors. An example of this is *Virgin Soil Upturned* by Mikhail Sholokhov, written in 1932. All mention of Stalin's rivals like Trotsky was written out of the history books and he himself was written up as Lenin's right-hand man in 1917.

The opposite of the command economy is the western system of free enterprise or private enterprise, where factories produce those goods and set the prices that the market will bear, i.e. that the customers will buy. Factories are judged not by output but by their ability to make a profit, i.e. whether or not people buy their goods. If a factory cannot make a profit, it goes bankrupt.

Annual production in the USSR

	1928	1940	
Electricity	5.0	48.3	milliard KWH
Oil	11.6	31.1	million tons
Coal	35.5	166.0	million tons
Gas	0.3	3.4	milliard cubic metres
Steel	4.3	18.3	million tons
Tractors	1.3	31.6	thousand units

Milliard: thousand millions.

The other motive for collectivization was to increase party control over the countryside. Machine Tractor Stations (MTS), run by loyal Communists, were set up to lend expensive machinery to *kolkhozes* that could not afford to buy it. Their job had as much to do with policing the countryside as helping agriculture.

To mechanize agriculture and increase output, farming was collectivized. Peasant farmers were ordered to pool their land, tools and animals to form collective farms or *kolkhozes*, which were worked communally, although they were also given small private plots to grow their own food on in their spare time. Annual production targets for each farm were set by the state and most of the produce was bought at fixed prices for export or to feed the growing towns. Farmers were expected now to work for the general good and not for their own personal gain and were paid according to the number of hours that they put in on the collective farm. Those who resisted were deported far away to the labour camps. Uncounted millions died. The results were disappointing. By 1940 production was up but not to the spectacular heights forecast by Stalin in 1928. The suspicion existed, even in Communist Party circles, that the peasants did not work as hard for the collective farms as they had done on their own.

The Soviet Union and the World

In *Mein Kampf* (1925) Hitler designated Soviet territory as *Lebensraum* (living space) for the German master-race.

Otherwise known as the Molotov-Ribbentrop Pact, after the Soviet and German Foreign Ministers who signed it.

It was the mission of all Communists to spread the Revolution throughout the world, but in the 1930s this dream took second place to the Soviet Union's need – as the world's only Communist state – to survive in a hostile, capitalist world. The danger became much worse in 1933 when Hitler came to power in Germany, for he had sworn to destroy both Communism and the Soviet Union. Desperately Stalin tried to cement a defensive alliance with the Western democracies, especially Britain and France. When this failed, he tried to buy time with the Nazi-Soviet Non-Aggression Pact of August 1939. While Hitler invaded the West in 1940, Stalin seized Eastern Poland, the Baltic States of Lithuania, Latvia and Estonia and part of southern Finland to make a buffer zone against the German attack that he feared would come one day. The events of the 1930s only confirmed the USSR's deep-seated and irradicable distrust of the West.

The Great Patriotic War

The Soviet name for the Second World War. The other popular name is 'The Great Fatherland War'.

The Germans invaded the Soviet Union on 22 June 1941 in Operation Barbarossa, and Russia became an ally of Britain and France (and later of the United States of America). For two years the war went disastrously for the Russians, with much of European Russia falling under German control. The turning point came at Stalingrad in January 1943, and by the time of the German surrender in May 1945 the Red Army occupied all of Europe east of the River Elbe, including Poland, Czechoslovakia, Hungary, Rumania, Bulgaria and the eastern parts of Germany and Austria.

The cost had been enormous. Between 20 and 25 million Soviet citizens were dead, a disproportionate number of them young adult males. In the 1950 census there were only 633 men for every 1000 women between the ages of 35 and 44. The women, children and old people left behind were weakened by the privations of war. Two-thirds of the infrastructure, factories and

Infrastructure: the basics of the economy such as roads, railways, bridges, dams etc, which do not themselves produce anything but make it possible for everything else to function.

A country in ruins. A burning village, set on fire as part of the 'scorched earth' policy followed by the Russians before German advances into Soviet territory, 1943.

Joseph Stalin.

Stalingrad, January 1943. The turning-point of the war. It was not for many years after the war that cities like this were rebuilt.

farmland of western Russia lay in ruins. So many houses had been destroyed that over 25 million people were homeless and living in cellars, caves or dugouts. The psychological impact may have been even greater. The memory of the invasion of 1941 and the western 'betrayal' that preceded it were etched for ever on the minds of a whole generation of Russians as proof that no capitalist state could ever be trusted, a distrust that was deepened by the revelation in August 1945 that the USA possessed an atomic bomb, which the Russians did not. If this is forgotten, much that happened after 1945 cannot be understood.

Sources for Soviet History

Sources for Soviet history have to be handled with care. The inner workings of government are kept far more secret than in more open societies, and, until recently, there has been little free expression of public opinion. The historian is forced to rely a great deal on official statements, which are often issued for propaganda purposes and do not tell the whole story. Some Western journalists who specialize in Soviet affairs are known as Kremlinologists because of their ability to read between the lines of official statements and work out what is really going on behind the scenes.

Conclusion

By 1945 the Soviet Union had moved a long way from the ideals of its founders 30 years before. The dream of socialist democracy had given way first to Party dictatorship and then to the iron rule of one man. During the chaos of the war years, there had been some relaxation of central control, as local areas and even individuals had been forced by circumstances to take the initiative into their own hand and contacts with the outside world had increased. But Stalin's prestige and his hold over the Party had emerged unshaken.

The Soviet Union came out of the war a Super-power, whose only military equal was the United States. Between them they held the future of Europe in their hands. But the victory was marred by the fear that the USSR was surrounded by enemies and by the enormous task of rebuilding the shattered country. It remained to be seen how Stalin would tackle these problems and newly won responsibilities.

Soviet troops in Berlin link up with their American counterparts, May 1945. Wartime comradeship was soon to turn into the hostility of the Cold War.

2 STALIN'S LAST YEARS: INSIDE THE USSR 1945-53

Stalin was 66 years old in 1945.

Khrushchev Remembers (Sphere Books, 1971), the memoirs of Nikita S. Khrushchev, illustrates vividly the fear in which Stalin was regarded by even his most powerful subordinates and how cravenly they rushed around obeying his every whim. *1984*, the famous novel by George Orwell, was based on his view of the USSR at this time.

Source A
From a speech made by Stalin at a meeting in Moscow during the elections to the Supreme Soviet, 9 February 1946.

Source B
From *A Russian Journal* by the American writer John Steinbeck (New York, 1948).

Introduction

If Soviet citizens hoped that the greater freedom and contact with the outside world of the war years would continue and that there would be no return to the total repression of the pre-war period, they were to be disappointed. Instead the aims and methods of the 1930s were revived in all areas of national life, sometimes – as in agriculture – with disastrous results. In retrospect, this was hardly surprising. Stalin was now an old man, set in his ways and terrified of invasion from the West. His colleagues were Party-men, who owed him their careers and would not openly question his judgement. The eight years between the end of the war and Stalin's death in March 1953 form a grim – and to the outside world little-known – postscript to the dramatic story of the Five-Year Plans and the Great Patriotic War.

Rebuilding Industry

What material potential did our country enjoy before the Second World War?

What policy permitted the Communist Party to provide this material potential in such a short time? First of all, the Soviet policy of industrialization of the country . . . . Secondly, the policy of the collectivization of agriculture . . . . Now for a few words about the plans of the Communist Party in the near future . . . the party intends to organize a new expansion of the economy which will make it possible for us, for example, to treble output compared with the pre-war period. We have to do this so that our industry can produce annually about 50 million tonnes of pig iron, about 60 million tonnes of steel, about 500 million tonnes of coal and about 60 million tonnes of oil. Only under these conditions can we consider that our Motherland will be protected against all accidents. This will take, let us say, three more Five-Year Plans, if not more. But this can be done and we must do it.

Our windows looked out on acres of rubble, broken brick and concrete and pulverized plaster, and in the wreckage the strange dark weeds that always seem to grow in destroyed places. During the time we were in Stalingrad we grew more and more fascinated with this expanse of ruin, for it was not deserted. Underneath the rubble were cellars and holes and in these holes many people lived. Stalingrad was a large city, and it had had apartment houses and many flats, and now it has none except a few on the outskirts, and its population has to live somewhere. It lives in the cellars of the buildings where the apartments once were.

??

1 How does Stalin in Source A envisage the post-war economic development of the USSR?

2 Why does he consider such a course necessary?

3 From the description in Source B, what do you think the greatest needs of the Soviet people may have been. Are these likely to be met in the near future?

The Fourth and Fifth Five-Year Plans (1946-50 and 1951-5) followed the pre-war model. They were centrally-planned, demanded almost superhuman effort from the depleted workforce and concentrated entirely on heavy industry. The strict labour laws were continued and a six-day working week of 10 to 12 hours a day was the norm. The results were dramatic. Despite all the difficulties, industrial output in 1950 – only five years after the end of the war – was 40 per cent higher than in 1940, enabling the Soviet Union to catch up with her military rival, the United States. The first Soviet atom bomb was successfully tested in 1949 and her first hydrogen bomb in 1953 – several months ahead of the Americans. Not only were the devastated Western regions re-industrialized, but important industrial belts opened in the vast Eastern territories like Siberia (iron and steel), Kazakhstan and Soviet Central Asia (textiles).

The recovery was aided by one-sided trade agreements imposed upon the satellite states of Eastern Europe. See p. 6.

Yet the plans had grave defects. Few consumer goods like clothing, footwear and household appliances were made and little new housing built. Living conditions for the majority of Soviet citizens improved little, if at all. Centralized planning meant that all decisions, even quite small ones, had to be approved by the planners in Moscow. A factory wanting to manufacture a new type of tractor, for example, had to get permission from at least eight different ministries before production could begin. This stifled initiative, as did the emphasis on increasing output as rapidly as possible. Factory managers tended to stick to the same old way of doing things rather than risk trying anything new. New inventions in plastics and chemicals, especially those which had been made in the West, were ignored. Scarce resources were used up in prestige projects like the new skyscraper office block in Moscow, which housed government offices. 'The shape of the recovery', wrote one historian, 'thus froze the Soviet economy back into the shape it had assumed in the Thirties' – while the rest of the world moved on.

A History of the Soviet Union, by G. Hosking (Fontana, 1985).

Alec Nove, an economist at a British University, tells of the time in 1955 when he met a Soviet agricultural delegation on a visit to England. They were impressed by the British small-wheeled tractors, which would have had many uses in the USSR. Yet, because the current party line favoured large caterpillar tractors, they dared not suggest introducing them there.

Rebuilding Agriculture

By 1945 the land of Western Russia, which before the war had produced over half the country's food, was ruined. Most of the livestock was dead and farm machinery destroyed. What agriculture there was was forced back on primitive methods, such as the use of human labour to pull ploughs. The shortage of young, fit men meant that as late as 1950 there were many villages whose only inhabitants were women and children, on whose shoulders fell all the heavy work. The grain harvest, which had been 95.6 tons in 1940, only reached 47 million in 1945.

During the war many collective farms had broken up, and the peasants had divided up the communal lands to farm as if they were their own, selling the produce privately on the black market. In September 1946 an order went out that all land taken over during the war be returned at once to the collective. Each area was to deliver fixed quota of grain, set in Moscow, for shipment to the towns. By 1953 most collectives had even been enlarged to encourage mechanization, dropping in number from 250,000 in 1946 to 97,000. A number of state farms of *sovkhozy* were set up, which specialized in one particular crop and paid their labourers a wage as in a factory. The Mechanical Tractor Stations were refounded.

Recovery was dreadfully slow, as the following figures show, and the country often came near to famine between 1945 and 1953.

Source: *An Economic History of the USSR* by Alec Nove (Pelican, 1978)

	1940	1947	1948	1949	1950	1951	1952
			(million tons)				
Grain	95.6	65.9	67.2	70.2	81.2	78.8	92.2
Potatoes	76.1	74.5	95.0	89.6	88.6	58.7	69.2
Cows	28.0	23.0	23.8	24.2	24.6	24.3	24.9

According to Khrushchev's Secret Speech (see p. 21), Stalin refused to listen to his colleagues when they tried to tell him about the desperate situation in the countryside, and totally disregarded the facts and figures put before him. Apparently he believed his own propaganda films which 'dressed up and beautified the existing situation in agriculture' (from Khrushchev's Secret Speech).

Lavrenty P. Beria (1899-1953). See Biographical Notes, p. 61.

The experiences of some of these POWs (as well as those of other categories of Gulag internees) can be found in *The Gulag Archipelago* by Alexander Solzhenitsyn (3 volumes, 1974-8), which was based on interviews with over 200 prisoners.

Andrei A. Zhdanov (1896-1948). See Biographical Notes, p. 62.

Among Zhdanov's chief victims were the famous composers, Shostakovitch, Prokofiev and Khachaturian, whose music was condemned as too 'cosmopolitan', and the Leningrad poetess, Anna Akhmatova, who wrote lyrical poetry about love and religion.

Lysenko's theory was that changes brought about in plants and animals by environmental factors such as extremes of temperature could then be passed on to their descendants. This theory was approved by Stalin as the correct 'Marxist' view of heredity, and Soviet scientists who disagreed were persecuted.

Source A
Khrushchev Remembers.

Marshal Nikolai Bulganin (1895-1975), member of the Politburo 1948-57, Defence Minister 1953-5 and Prime Minister 1955-7. See chapter 4.

Almost no investment was made in re-equipping the farms with new machinery, rebuilding the roads and storehouses that had been destroyed or in new methods of breeding livestock. With productivity so low, farmers often had little left for themselves after they had delivered their quotas, and lived in semi-starvation and poverty. But so long as the towns were fed, Stalin ignored the problems of the countryside. We know from the memoirs of his successor, Khrushchev, that many top party men were desperately worried about the situation, but while Stalin lived there was little hope that anything would change.

The Closed Society

Contact with the outside world between 1941 and 1945 must have caused many Russians to question the myth that their society was perfect, but as the war drew to a close, the totalitarian apparatus of the Thirties was reimposed. The secret police – now under Lavrenty Beria – kept a close watch on people and party alike. All possibility of independent thought was stifled, as was any information that might call into question the wisdom of Stalin's judgement. Newspapers and books were censored, not only for opinions but also uncomfortable facts. Contacts with the outside world were shut off and many of those who had been 'contaminated' by such contacts disappeared into the labour camps of the Gulag, including high-ranking officers who had liaised with the Western allies and thousands of ordinary soldiers who had been prisoners of war in Germany. By 1953 the population of these camps was estimated at 8 million.

Until his death in 1948 responsibility for cultural affairs rested with Andrei Zhdanov. In a purge known as the Zhdanovshchina, he cleaned Soviet arts of everything that did not serve the aims of the state, such as cosmopolitanism (interest in things foreign), apoliticism (failure to write things that would serve the political aims of the state) and objectivism (the publication of facts that did not fit the current party line). One of the most remarkable features of this period was the absolute denial that anything good could come from outside the Soviet Union, even when this flew in the face of facts. Everything from steam engines to jet aircraft was supposed to have been invented by Russians, past or present. The theories of the biologist, Lysenko, regarded by nearly all scientists as nonsense, were preferred to new ideas about the chromosome as the basis of heredity, a theory which had come from the West. It was not until Stalin's death that Soviet scientists were once again allowed contact with international academic research.

Bulganin once described very well the experience we all had to live with in those days. We were leaving Stalin's after dinner one night and he said, You come to Stalin's table as a friend, but you never know if you'll go home by yourself or if you'll be given a ride – to prison.

Source B

The First Circle by Alexander Solzhenitsyn (Fontana, 1970). The scene here takes place in a girls' dormitory at the University of Moscow. The girls are discussing the difficulties they are having in completing their theses.

L.P. Beria in 1950.

'Oh, you have to weed out the foreigners, do you? Well, you're not the only one. Don't let that get you down'. Weeding out the foreigners meant going through the thesis throwing out every reference to a foreigner: 'As Lowe has shown', for example, would have to read, 'As scientists have shown' . . . . On the other hand, if a Russian had done anything at all to distinguish himself, then you had to give his full name and duly bring out his great patriotism and immortal services to science. 'No', replied Nadya, 'I got rid of the foreigners long ago. Now I have to throw out Academician B and the whole of his theory. I'd built the whole thesis around it. And now it turns out that he . . . .' Academician B had now been hurled into the same abyss as Nadya's husband.

? ?

1 What does Source A tell us about the position of top Party men in the USSR during this period? What effect would this have on the way the USSR was run?

2 Why are the girls in source B having such problems? How is it possible to guess accurately during which period this novel is set?

3 What do you think has happened to Academician B. and Nadya's husband? What possible reasons might there be?

The official view. A wise father of his people, Stalin signs state papers, watched by two picturesque delegates from the Tadzhik and Turkmen Soviet Republics in Central Asia.

The Last Days of Stalin

Stalin spent his last years creating around himself an atmosphere of fear and intrigue. There was no security even for his closest colleagues, who were afraid to speak their minds. By playing one top party member off against another, he made sure that no rival would ever challenge his own unique position. Zhdanov fell from favour in 1948 and died soon afterwards of a heart attack. Malenkov's star rose. Molotov, who had long been Foreign Minister, was increasingly cold-shouldered and his wife was sent to a camp. Beria, who was feared and loathed by all his colleagues, used his NVKD to amass a power-base second only to Stalin's. But of the plots and counter-plots that lay behind these sudden changes in fortune little reliable information can be discovered.

In January 1953 *Pravda* announced that nine doctors had been accused of murdering top Soviet leaders including Zhdanov. The NVKD was criticized for its incompetence in failing to uncover the plot in time, and it is likely that these were the opening moves in a campaign to discredit and oust Beria, who was becoming too powerful. Before this could happen Stalin himself died of an apparent brain haemorrhage following a stroke.

Conclusion

For 30 years Stalin had dominated and shaped Soviet society. He had converted a backward nation into a military and industrial giant but the cost in human suffering had been great and he had left serious problems for his successors, including a low standard of living and an under-productive agriculture. And the political future itself was far from certain, for his death was almost certain to be followed by a power struggle among the top Party men. And no one knew what the outcome would be.

Georgy M. Malenkov (1902-1988), member of Politburo since 1948 and widely regarded as Stalin's most likely successor. For his later career, see chapter 4 and Biographical Notes.

Vyacheslav Molotov (1890-1985). See Biographical Notes.

Inevitably, it was rumoured that Stalin had been murdered. There is no definite proof of this and he was 74 and had already had a stroke. The issue must remain undecided.

Sir Isaiah Berlin, Stalin's biographer, said of him that he 'found Russia working with a wooden plough and left her equipped with atomic piles'.

3 THE SUPERPOWER: THE USSR AND THE WORLD 1945-53

Introduction

World War II broke the power of Europe over world affairs. By the end Germany was defeated and devastated, Britain exhausted and Eastern Europe in ruins. The Japanese victories in the East in 1941 and 1942 had weakened Europe's hold over her colonial empires in Africa and Asia, ushering in an era of struggles for independence that was to last into the 1970s. The fate of the world now rested in the hands of the two nations who came out of the war the strongest – the new Superpowers, the USSR and the United States. The USA was economically far stronger and possessed the atomic bomb, but the Soviet Union, with 11 million men under arms, was the greatest conventional military power and controlled most of Eastern Europe, which had been liberated by the Red Army in 1944 and 1945. They had fought as allies during the war, but their social and political systems and visions of the post-war world were very different. The stage was set for a new conflict.

The Creation of the Soviet Empire in Eastern Europe

We must now be interested in supporting the national (Lublin) Committee and all who are . . . cooperating with it . . . . For the Soviet Union, which is bearing the whole burden of the struggle for freeing Poland from Germany, the problem of relations with Poland is . . . a matter of . . . close and friendly relations with an authority . . . which has already grown strong and has armed forces of its own . . . .

The Soviet Union, more than any other power, has a stake in strengthening a democratic Poland because Poland borders on the Soviet Union and because the Polish problem is inseparable from that of the security of the Soviet Union.

With frankness equal to your own I must tell you that I see no prospect of this Government's following suit . . . . Neither the Government nor the people of the United States have seen any evidence . . . to justify the conclusion that the Lublin Committee represents the people of Poland . . . . No opportunity to express themselves in regard to the Lublin Committee has yet been afforded to the people of Poland.

? ?

In 1945 colonies conquered by the Japanese, such as Malaya, Singapore and Burma (British), Indo-China (French) or the Dutch East Indies, were returned to the former colonial rulers.

Conventional military power: all non-nuclear troops and weapons.

The USA believed in democracy and the free enterprise economy.

Source A
A letter from Stalin to President Franklin Roosevelt of the USA, 27 December 1944.

Lublin Committee: a group of Polish Communists, most of whom had spent the war in the USSR. The Red Army installed them in the city of Lublin as the new government of Poland in late 1944.

Democratic: in Communist terminology 'democracy' usually means only 'socialist democracy' and not the kind practised in many western nations.

Source B
Roosevelt's reply to Stalin, 31 December 1944.

Soviet allies in Eastern Europe after 1945.

1 What is the main difference of opinion between the USSR and the USA over the future of Poland? How is this reflected in their differing interpretations of democracy?

2 How can this divergence be explained?

3 In the circumstances of late 1944, who was most likely to get his own way and why?

The shock of the German invasion of 1941 dominated Soviet thinking after the war. To prevent such an event from recurring the political map of Eastern Europe must be redrawn to create a buffer zone of friendly states around her western frontier and Germany must never be allowed to regain her pre-war military strength. Such a unique opportunity to mould events in the Soviet Union's interests might never occur again.

As the war drew to a close the Baltic States, East Prussia, Byelorussia, Poland east of the River Vistula and part of south-east Finland were annexed to the USSR. Between 1945 and 1948, in collusion with the local Communist Parties, Communist régimes were imposed upon Poland, Bulgaria, Rumania, Hungary and Czechoslovakia, usually against the will of the majority of the inhabitants. Under the watchful eyes of the Red Army, elections were rigged, the press and radio stations taken over and non-Communist members of coalition governments hounded out of office. In Hungary, for example, the Communist Party under Matyas Ragosi won only 17 per cent of the votes in the free election of November 1945 but were given the key posts of Minister of the Interior (which controlled the police) and Minister of Information (which controlled the mass media). Over the next two years Hungary was transformed into a one-party Communist state.

The new Communist states of Eastern Europe were named Peoples' Democracies. Nominally independent, all their activities were, in fact, tightly controlled from Moscow through the Communist Information Bureau or COMINFORM, set up in 1947. All of them had Soviet secret policemen and soldiers stationed on their territories. A Red Army Marshal, Rokossovsky, was even appointed Polish Defence Minister. Economic life was modelled closely on the Soviet pattern, including crash industrialization programmes and the collectivization of agriculture. The COMECON, set up in 1949, made sure that most of their trade was with the Soviet Union, and that it worked to the Russians' advantage. Any signs of unrest among local communists at this total subservience to the USSR were stamped out by ruthless purges. In 1952 many of the Czech party leaders, including the General Secretary, Rudolf Slansky and Foreign Minister, Vladimir Clementis, were executed after show-trials. In the West, Eastern Europe became known as the Soviet Bloc or the 'satellite states'. In 1949 they were joined by the Soviet zone of Germany, now the German Democratic Republic or East Germany.

The USSR and the West

The war-time alliance between the USSR and the capitalist West, always fraught with mistrust, soon fell apart. At the Yalta conference in February 1945 Stalin had promised free elections in Eastern Europe and broken his word soon afterwards. At Potsdam in July and August the Soviet leader and the new American President, Harry S. Truman, clashed over the future of Poland, which was already being converted into a Soviet satellite, and over the adoption of the Oder–Neisse line as the new Polish frontier with Germany. During the conference Truman received news that an atomic bomb had been successfully tested in the New Mexican desert. He told Churchill, the British Prime Minister, but not Stalin. Three weeks later on 6 August the first bomb was dropped on Hiroshima.

In the months that followed, as the Soviet grip on Eastern Europe tightened, East-West co-operation in occupied Germany also broke down. Stalin refused to allow free elections to be held as a prelude to reunification, unless Communist representation in the new government could be guaranteed. He demanded heavy reparations from Germany, which the West was not prepared to concede. To many in the West, including Truman, it appeared that the USSR was intent on world conquest and would be stopped only by force. In March 1946 Churchill made a speech at Fulton, Missouri, warning his audience that an 'iron curtain' had fallen across Europe and that preparations must be made to ward off 'Communist aggression'. From the Soviet point of view, things looked very different.

A Polish joke of the time asked: 'What is the new animal invented by Comrade Stalin?' Answer: 'A cross between a cow and a giraffe. It grazes in Poland but is milked in the USSR'.

Harry S. Truman, President of the USA 1945-52.

The Soviet Union had annexed part of Eastern Poland. To compensate Poland, who was being drawn into the Soviet bloc and was therefore a friendly nation, the Polish-German frontier was moved westward to the line of the rivers Oder and Neisse. This was not accepted by the USA until the 1970s.

It had been agreed to divide Germany and her capital, Berlin, into four temporary zones of occupation – one for each of the four big Allies. It was intended to reunify the country eventually. The same arrangements had been made for Austria and her capital, Vienna. Both Berlin and Vienna were inside the Soviet zone and special routes were designated to allow the West access to their sectors through Soviet territory.

Reparations: compensation for losses.

Source A
Khrushchev Remembers, p. 197.

The Potsdam agreement was a one-sided agreement, particularly as it affected Berlin and Vienna. These cities were located in the zone occupied by Soviet troops, and it would have seemed that they should be part of our zone. However, the allies didn't give them to us. Berlin and Vienna were each divided into four sectors. We received one sector, and the Western powers – England, America and France – received the other three. This says something about the distribution of power at the end of the war.

Source B
A remark by Stalin made in a conversation with the American ambassador, Walter Bedell Smith in March 1946, from *My Three Years in Moscow* by W. Bedell Smith (Philadelphia, 1950).

We cannot for one minute forget the basic truth that our country remains the one socialist state in the world . . . . The victory we achieved in the war does not mean that all dangers to our state structure and social order have disappeared. I am convinced that the capitalist nations will not rest until they have destroyed us.

Source C
Stalin, in an interview in the Soviet newspaper, *Pravda*, 14 March 1946.

Basically Mr Churchill has taken up the position of a warmonger. And Mr Churchill is not alone in this. He has friends not only in England but also in the United States.

It should be mentioned that Mr Churchill and his friends are strikingly reminiscent in this respect of Hitler and his friends.

? ?

1 From what Khrushchev says in Source A, how did the USSR feel about its position in the world at the end of the war? Does it explain future Soviet behaviour over Eastern Europe and Germany?

2 In what context were Stalin's remarks in Sources B and C made? What can we tell from them about the Soviet interpretation of Western motives in the post-war period?

3 Can the West be justified for seeing things differently? Was one side more to blame than the other for the breakdown in relations?

The Federal Republic of Germany (West Germany) was established in May 1949. The German Democratic Republic (East Germany) was established in October 1949.

NATO: North Atlantic Treaty Organization, a mutual defence pact against Communism signed by 11 Western nations including the USA and Britain in April 1949. Later joined by Greece, Turkey and Portugal (1952) and West Germany (1955). Both conventional troops and nuclear weapons were installed on territory close to the Soviet border, including northern Norway, Turkey and north-west Canada. Although NATO's stated purpose is defensive, it has looked threatening to the Russians ever since. One present-day Western journalist has written: 'for an American to understand Soviet fears of encirclement, he would have to imagine Soviet bases all along the Canadian and Mexican borders.' (Martin Walker, *The Waking Giant*, Sphere Books, 1988).

East versus West

By 1947 the two sides were locked in conflict over the future of Europe. The first climax came when the Western allies introduced a new currency into their zones of Germany and Berlin. Stalin saw this as the opening move in a scheme to draw Germany into the Western camp and retaliated by blocking all the access routes into the three Western sectors of Berlin. For 11 months, from June 1948 until May 1949, the Allies supplied West Berlin by air, until the Russians admitted defeat and called the blockade off. By 1949 Germany was divided into two separate states and all hope of reunification was dead. When NATO was formed the USSR saw herself finally surrounded by a ring of hostile capitalist states. The Cold War had begun.

Stalin's distrust of the West was now irradicable and he often spoke of the inevitability of a war-to-the-finish between capitalism and communism. East-West relations went on deteriorating down to his death in 1953. A deadly arms race began. In 1953 the Soviet Union still had over three million men under arms, and both Super-powers were on the way to developing a hydrogen bomb, ten times more powerful than the bomb dropped on Hiroshima.

Stalin and Tito

The USSR's complete hold over Eastern Europe was broken in 1948 by the small nation of Yugoslavia. In 1944-5 Yugoslav Communist partisans under the leadership of Tito liberated their country themselves without help from the Red Army and set up a popular Communist government, which owed

Marshal Tito: real name Josip Broz. Founder member of Yugoslav Communist Party, leader of Partisans 1941-5, and ruler of Yugoslavia until his death in 1980.

Source A

From COMINFORM's denunciation of Tito, June 1948.

Source B

Milovan Djilas, *Conversations with Stalin* (Pelican, 1969). Djilas was a Yugoslav Communist, close colleague of Tito and a member of the delegation which went to Moscow in January 1948 to put the Yugoslav case. This was the third time he had met and talked privately with Stalin and it put the seal on his growing disillusionment with Soviet-style Communism.

Non-aligned: neutral in the Cold War, belonging to neither the Eastern nor Western bloc.

nothing to the Russians. At first the two nations were allies and Yugoslavia joined COMINFORM, but by 1948 they had fallen out. Their disagreements were many. Tito resisted Soviet attempts to impose one-sided trade agreements and to recruit Yugoslav citizens into the NKVD to act as spies in their own country. Stalin was angered by Tito's refusal to collectivize agriculture on the Soviet model and by his plans for closer economic cooperation with neighbouring Bulgaria, which had been drawn up without prior consultation with the USSR. The real reason for the quarrel ran deeper.

No one can deny the merits of the Yugoslav Communist Party but they are no greater than those of the CPs of Poland, Czechoslovakia etc. . . . . Yet the leaders of these parties are modest and do not set their own opinions against those of their comrades and split everybody's ears, the way the Yugoslavs do with their boasting . . . . In refusing to attend the COMINFORM meeting, the Yugoslav leaders are dodging the just criticism of the fraternal parties . . . the leadership of the Communist Party of Yugoslavia has broken with the Party's international tradition and embarked on a cause of selfish nationalism.

Stalin's support for revolutions was conditional, so long as they did not go beyond the interests of the Soviet state. He felt instinctively that the creation of revolutionary centres outside Moscow would endanger its supremacy in world Communism, and of course that is what actually happened. That is why he helped revolutions up to a certain point – as long as he could control them – but he was always ready to leave them in the lurch whenever they slipped out of his grasp . . . in his own country Stalin had subjected all activities to his views and to his personality, so he could not behave differently outside.

? ?

1 In Source A, what is COMINFORM really accusing the Yugoslav Communists of doing?

2 How does Djilas's interpretation of events differ from that of COMINFORM? If Djilas is right about Stalin's attitude towards revolutions, how is this likely to affect his relations with Communist parties elsewhere in the world?

3 Why did the Yugoslavs, alone among the Communist parties of Eastern Europe, dare to take such an independent stand and how did they get away with it.

Yugoslavia was expelled from COMINFORM and all Soviet aid withdrawn. If Stalin had hoped that economic collapse would force Tito back into line, he miscalculated. Tito survived to develop his own unique brand of Yugoslav communism and to establish her in world affairs as a non-aligned state. The example of Yugoslavia's successful defiance of her powerful neighbour may have been a significant cause of the wave of unrest that swept through the satellite states after Stalin's death.

The USSR and the World

During the war the Communist duty to spread the revolution was played down, but now it was revived as a weapon in the Cold War battle for the hearts and minds of the peoples of the world. Everywhere local Communist parties looked to the USSR as a guide and inspiration and were natural allies in the struggle to undermine the capitalist nations and their empires.

In 1950 a Treaty of Mutual Friendship and Assistance was signed with the

The Cold War hots up. US Forces in the South Korean capital of Seoul, Korean War, 1950.

The Korean War (1950-53) was between Communist North Korea and the non-Communist South, which was backed by the USA. In his memoirs Khrushchev claims that the invasion was the idea of Kim Il-sung, the North Korean leader, but that he consulted Stalin first and gained his approval.

India and Pakistan became independent in 1947, Burma in 1948 and Indonesia (the former Dutch East Indies) in 1949. There were violent independence struggles in Indo-China 1945-54 and Malaya. In the 1950s nationalist movements grew up rapidly in all parts of colonial Africa. In 1954 Indo-China became independent as the separate countries Laos, Cambodia (Kampuchea), Communist North Vietnam and non-Communist South. This was the background to the Vietnam War (see chapter 7).

Chinese Civil War (1946-9) between the Communists and the Kuomintang (Nationalists).

Chinese Communists under Mao Zedong, who had come to power in 1949. Generous economic aid was sent to help China become industrialized. The USSR backed the North Koreans during the Korean War of 1950-3, supplying most of their tanks and planes, although whether the North's attack on the South was actually instigated by the Russians, as the West claimed, remains uncertain.

But the success of Soviet policy abroad was often hampered by Stalin's inability, described by Djilas, to work with anyone that he could not totally control. Aid was refused, for example, to all non-Communists, even when their activities might help the Soviet cause. The first COMINFORM meeting in 1948 almost ignored the nationalist movements that were growing up in Africa and Asia. As with Yugoslavia, even fellow Communists were distrusted unless they slavishly followed instructions from Moscow, as the East Europeans had been forced to do. No help was sent to the independent-minded Vietnamese Communist Ho Chi Minh in his fight against the French colonial government, nor had any been sent to the Chinese before 1949. Stalin's inflexibility may have lost the USSR golden opportunities in the Cold War struggle for the hearts and minds of the peoples of the world.

Conclusion

At the time of Stalin's death the Soviet Union was locked in a conflict with the United States that seemed destined one day to end in a major war. Western politicians blamed the tension on Soviet lust for world conquest, but the generation of Russians who had lived through the Great Patriotic War were motivated as much by fear as by aggression. At the same time some top Soviet leaders (as became apparent after 1953) were becoming aware just how dangerous this deadlock was. The Cold War and the arms race were eating up a lion's share of the USSR's economic wealth, and now that both Super-powers had nuclear weapons it was increasingly likely that a war between them would leave no victor.

4 AFTER STALIN: DESTALINIZATION 1953~8

Deify: to give the status of a god.

Deification. Members of the Politburo (including Molotov, second right and Beria, right) carry the body en route to the Lenin Mausoleum.

Introduction

At his death Stalin was deified. His body was buried with Lenin's in the mausoleum in Red Square, where it could become a place of pilgrimage. His obituary referred to him as 'Lenin's comrade-in-arms, the standard-bearer of his genius, the wise leader and teacher of the Communist Party and the Soviet Union'. Within three years, however, his god-like image had been shattered, not by enemies but by the new leaders of the Communist Party itself. How and why this came about and what it meant for the Soviet Union and the world is the subject of this chapter.

The term 'thaw' was taken from the novel called *The Thaw* by Ilya Ehrenburg, which was published in the magazine *Novy Mir* ['New World'] in 1954. It means a *relaxation* or *lessening of tension*.

The 'own roads to socialism' theory made a great impact on the satellite states.

Source A
Extracts from Khrushchev's speech to the 20th Party Congress, as published by the US government, 4 June 1956. No official version was ever published in the USSR.

Source B
From the West German satirical magazine, *Simplicissimus*, showing Khrushchev 'crowning' Stalin with the corpses of victims of purges and persecutions.

The Thaw at Home

The top Party men, who had lived in fear of their lives for so long, were determined that never again should one of them become all-powerful. They arranged a collective leadership. Malenkov became Chairman of the Council of Ministers (Prime Minister) and Khrushchev was Party Secretary. Some of the most blatant aspects of Stalinist terror were ended. By the summer Beria had been sacked, secretly tried and shot. The powers of the NKVD were reduced and it was renamed the Committee of State Security or KGB. Many of the surviving inmates of the Labour camps were released. The absolute stranglehold of Socialist Realism on the arts was relaxed a little to allow the publication of more honest novels like Ehrenburg's *The Thaw* or Vladimir Dudintsev's *Not by Bread Alone*, which pointed out that many party officials were petty-minded and even corrupt. For the first time party officials admitted in public that Soviet agriculture was far from healthy and that living standards were too low. The unnecessary quarrel with Yugoslavia, which had arisen from Stalin's inability to tolerate any view but his own, was patched up. A Soviet delegation, which included Khrushchev, visited Belgrade in 1955, apologized for the USSR's behaviour in 1948 and acknowledged Yugoslavia's right to find her own road to socialism.

The 'Secret Speech'

A party congress – the 20th – was held in February 1956. Here Party Secretary Khrushchev made a historic speech. It was meant only for the ears of the delegates but its contents soon leaked out to the people of the USSR and to the world.

Stalin showed in a whole series of cases his intolerance, his brutality and his abuse of power . . . he often chose the path of repression and physical annihilation, not only against actual enemies, but also against individuals who had not committed any crimes against the Party and the Soviet government . . . when the cases of some of these . . . were examined it was found that all their cases were fabricated. Confessions of guilt of many arrested and charged were gained with the help of cruel and inhuman tortures.
. . . It is impermissible and foreign to the spirit of Marxism-Leninism to elevate one person, to transform him into a superman possessing supernatural characteristics akin to those of a god. Such a man supposedly knows everything, sees everything, thinks for everyone, can do anything, is infallible in his behaviour.
Such belief about a man, and specifically about Stalin, was cultivated among us for many years.

Khrushchev also criticized Stalin's conduct of the war, blaming him for the disasters of the early months, and then for taking on himself most of the credit for the final victory. He also read out Lenin's testament, which was highly critical of Stalin, and which had been suppressed ever since the former's death in 1924.

? ?

1 What does Khrushchev accuse Stalin of in these extracts from the secret speech?

2 Do you think Khrushchev is telling the full story here or are there important things that he has left out or glossed over?

For events in Hungary and Poland in 1956, see p. 24.

Khrushchev read out protests of innocence that had been written to Stalin by top party men before their execution and never delivered. These had been found in the files of the NKVD. But he made no mention of groups like Kulaks or the returning prisoners of war.

Tsaritsyn on the River Volga had been renamed Stalingrad in 1925. In 1942-3 it was the site of one of the most famous battles of World War II. In 1956 it was renamed Volgograd, the name it still bears today. Stalin's daughter, Svetlana, recalls how plans to make her father's dacha (country cottage) into a museum in his honour were dropped after the 20th Party Congress and the house shut up.

Khrushchev's defeated rivals were given honorable jobs in remote parts of the USSR, where they could not meddle in politics. Molotov became Soviet ambassador to Mongolia and Malenkov was made director of a hydro-electric power station in Kazakstan.

Andrei A. Gromyko (1909-1989): Foreign Minister of USSR 1957-1985, throughout all of the period covered by chapters 5, 6, and 7 of this book.

In the West Khrushchev was often known as Chairman Khrushchev.

Whatever the disagreements behind the scenes in the Politburo, a façade of unity was always put on in public. For the events surrounding Khrushchev's downfall, see p. 34.

In the aftermath of the speech waves of both shock and excitement swept the Soviet Union and Eastern Europe, for much that Russians had been taught to believe for the past 20 or so years was now called into question. Khrushchev's accusations, however, were as significant for what they left out as for what they revealed. There was no mention of the non-party victims of the Terror, and no criticism of the dramatic changes that had taken place before the late 1930s. The basis of the Soviet state, including collectivized agriculture and the right of the party to control the lives of 200 million Soviet citizens was left intact. If life got better for most people after 1956, it did not get much freer. And of Khrushchev's own rise to the top by stepping in dead men's shoes no hint was made. The secret speech, it now seems clear, was a move by Khrushchev in the power struggle going on behind the walls of the Kremlin, although its exact role is still not clear. It may also have been intended to whitewash Khrushchev's reputation by heaping all the blame for the purges on to one man.

Stalin's name, though, almost disappeared from the official record. The countless towns and streets named after him were renamed yet again. His role in Soviet history was downgraded. At the 1961 Party Congress he was denounced yet again and his body was removed from the mausoleum and reburied inside the Kremlin walls, marked only by a simple plaque.

The Rise of Khrushchev

Like Stalin before him, Khrushchev used the influential position of Party Secretary to out-manouevre his political rivals. He engineered the dismissal of Malenkov in 1955 and replaced him with his own supporter, Marshal Bulganin. His 1956 destalinization speech helped to discredit former colleagues, while leaving his own reputation unstained. In June 1957, while Khrushchev was in Finland, his enemies in the Politburo, including Malenkov and Molotov, conspired to oust him. He flew home in haste and insisted on a meeting of the full Party Central Committee, which had long since been packed with his supporters. It voted overwhelmingly in his favour. Molotov and Malenkov were sacked from the Politburo and their political careers were over. But unlike Stalin's rivals, their lives were not threatened. Their places were taken by men loyal to Khrushchev, including Andrei Gromyko, who replaced Molotov as foreign minister. Nine months later Bulganin too was dismissed and Khrushchev became Chairman of the council of Ministers as well, just as Stalin had been.

Things were not the same, however. Although Khrushchev was to become increasingly egotistical over the years, he never cowed the party as Stalin had done. To stay in power, he was always dependent on its approval, and Kremlinologists have concluded that a number of bitter disputes over policy went on behind the scenes between 1957 and 1964, when Khrushchev was ousted by his colleagues. His style and personality were quite different from Stalin's, for Khrushchev was gregarious and remained close to his roots among the factory workers and peasants. Willing to listen to people and learn about their problems, he never lost touch with reality. More flexible than Stalin, he was willing to experiment with different solutions to the USSR's chronic agricultural and industrial problems, even though he never questioned the basic Communist principles of state and party control.

The Thaw Abroad

Relations with the rest of the world were also reappraised after Stalin's death.

Source A
From a speech made by Khrushchev at the 20th Party Congress, February 1956.

Source B
From a speech by deputy Foreign Minister, Shepilov, at the 20th Party Congress, February 1956.

The simultaneous existence of two opposite world economic systems, the capitalist and socialist, developing according to different laws and in opposite directions, has become an indisputable fact . . . . The Leninist principle of peaceful co-existence of states with different social systems has always been and remains the general line of our country's foreign policy . . . . And this is natural, for there is no other way in present-day conditions. Indeed there are only two ways: either peaceful coexistence or the most destructive war in history. There is no third way.

Peaceful coexistence is not a conflictless life. As long as different social-political systems exist, the antagonisms between them are unavoidable. Peaceful coexistence is a struggle, political, economic and ideological . . . . Coexistence means that one does not fight the other, does not attempt to solve international disputes by force of arms, but that one competes through peaceful work and economic and cultural activities. But we would cease to be Marxist-Leninists if we forgot the elementary laws of class struggle.

? ?

1 In what way does Khrushchev's idea of peaceful coexistence in Source A mark a break with Stalin's attitude towards the capitalist world? Why was it necessary?

2 What does Source B tell us about the meaning of peaceful coexistence?

3 How might the new policy alter Soviet attitudes towards the West, the satellite states and the Third World?

A final peace treaty has never been signed and Korea remains divided into two opposing states.

Summit conference: meeting between the leaders of the Super-powers. Present at Geneva were Khrushchev and Bulganin, President Eisenhower of USA, Prime Minister Anthony Eden of Britain and Prime Minister Faure of France.

Dwight D. Eisenhower (1890-1969): Supreme Allied Commander 1943-5 and President of the USA 1952-60.

Verify: check up (that the treaty obligation had been kept).

Some outstanding disputes with the West were settled. Four months after Stalin's death an armistice halted fighting in Korea. A peace treaty was signed with Austria and the four-power occupation ended. Soviet troops were withdrawn from Southern Finland, where they had been stationed since 1944. Contacts with the West were resumed. Khrushchev and Bulganin visited Britain in 1956. In the summer of 1955 the first summit conference since Potsdam was held, in Geneva, although no agreement was reached on the key questions of disarmament and Germany. This period was known as the 'Thaw'.

On the vital questions affecting Soviet security, however, Stalin's successors were as unbending as he had been, for they too had lived through the events of 1941-5. At the Geneva Summit they refused once again to accept elections as an essential prelude to the reunification of Germany, and divided Berlin remained the focus of world-wide debate. In rivalry to NATO, the Warsaw Pact was created in 1955 to co-ordinate the armed forces of the USSR and the satellite states. Negotiations to restrict the development of nuclear weapons foundered on Soviet refusal to allow inspection of her military installations. In 1955 President Eisenhower's Open Skies Plan, which would have allowed each Super-power to fly over the territory of the other to verify whether arms limitation agreements were being complied with, was rejected as too dangerous to Soviet security. The deadly and expensive arms race went on, so too did support for Communist parties abroad.

Revolution in Hungary

Destalinization made its greatest impact on Eastern Europe, where Communism was associated with foreign domination and people joked grimly that their leaders had been brought into the country 'on the back of a Red Army truck'. Only three months after Stalin's death in June 1953, a general strike broke out in East Berlin, which had to be quelled by Soviet troops.

Wladyslaw Gomulka (1905-1982): Polish Communist, who had fought in Polish resistance during the war and maintained a degree of independence from Stalinist policies. Purged and imprisoned in 1948 and only released in 1955. Removed from party leadership in 1970.

Autonomy: self-government. This included a privileged position for the Roman Catholic Church.

Imre Nagy (1896-1958). Nagy had briefly been Prime Minister in 1953, when he had begun a cautious destalinization. In 1955 he had been ousted in a come-back by hard-line Stalinists under Rakosi but had remained popular with the people, who demanded his reinstatement in October 1956. After the Soviet invasion of November he sought refuge in the Yugoslav embassy, from which he was lured out by promise of a pardon. He was tried in secret in Rumania in 1958 and shot.

Janos Kadar (1912-): he had been purged during the Rakosi period and served as a member of Nagy's government, but then changed sides to support the Soviet invasion. Secretary of the Hungarian Communist party until he was sacked in 1988.

Cracks appear in the Soviet Empire. Riots in Budapest, October 1956.

Source A
From *Budapest 1956* by Miklos Molnar (1971). In 1956 the author was editor of the magazine published by the Hungarian Writers' Union and experienced the events of October and November at first hand.

Source B
Khrushchev to Egyptian Vice-President, Anwar Sadat, in 1964. Quoted in *The Sphinx and the Commissar* by Mohammed Heikal, (Collins 1978).

Source C
Khrushchev in a conversation with the Yugoslav ambassador, Veljko Micunovic, 25 October 1956. Quoted in *Moscow Diary*, by V. Micunovic (Chatto and Windus, 1980).

The promise that Yugoslavia would be allowed to find her own road to socialism, followed by Khrushchev's secret speech, brought tensions to a head in 1956. In June, after protests by Polish workers against both the low standard of living and the repressive government, the USSR allowed Bierut, the leader of the Polish Communist Party, to be replaced by the more popular Wladyslaw Gomulka, and Poland was given a much greater degree of cultural and economic autonomy.

In the autumn a similar train of events began in Hungary. Demonstrating students and workers forced the removal of the Stalinists, Rakosi and Gero, and their replacement as Party Secretary by Imre Nagy. Swept along by popular demand, Nagy all but abolished censorship, freed political prisoners and dropped restrictions on travel abroad. Open talk began of turning Hungary into a multi-party state and even withdrawing from the Warsaw Pact, which would have taken Hungary out of the Soviet bloc altogether. Defence minister Rokossovsky was sent home. On 4 November Soviet tanks were sent into the capital, Budapest. After a few days of street fighting, in which as many as 20,000 may have died, the Hungarian 'rebellion' was crushed. The Russians installed Janos Kadar, whom they trusted, as Party Secretary.

When the speeches made in Moscow were published, the effect hit Hungarian life like a stone falling on a wasps' nest. In the universities, offices and factories, the people, silent until that moment, began to discuss feverishly what it might mean for Hungary .... The hold of the Communist Party over the minds of the people began to disintegrate.

Molotov thought that it was my policies that led to trouble in Hungary . . . and that my tolerance of Tito had encouraged the Hungarians.

Anti-Soviet elements have taken up arms against the camp of the Soviet Union . . . . The West is seeking a revision of the results of World War II and has started in Hungary, and will then go on to crush each socialist state in Europe one by one.

???

1 From the evidence in Sources A and B, why do you think the Hungarians felt they might get away with their virtual withdrawal from the Soviet bloc in 1956? What other recent events might have given them encouragement?

2 How does Khrushchev's interpretation of the Hungarian situation in Source C differ from that in source A? Is it likely to be an honest view?

3 What do you think were the real reasons for Soviet intervention in Hungary in 1956?

The events of 1956 taught East Europeans that no Soviet ruler would accept changes that threatened her security and her hold over the satellite states. At the same time the USSR learned that to keep her bloc under control by brute force was both expensive and damaging to her reputation abroad. It would be easier to buy off popular discontent with more prosperity and cultural freedom, as was already happening in Poland. Hungary, for example, was afterwards allowed to develop an economy based partly on private enterprise, which by the 1970s gave her the highest standard of living in Eastern Europe.

Conclusion

In the five years after Stalin's death great changes had begun in all the lands under Soviet rule. As the shadow of the terror lifted, there was hope of a better future, although many grave problems, especially economic ones, remained to be solved. But events in Hungary had shown that the USSR's new rulers would be as ruthless in defence of Soviet interests as ever Stalin had been. And while the Communist Party remained supreme, the freedoms it had granted could just as easily be taken away again. There was no guarantee that another Stalin would not emerge. A few years later, writing as Stalin's body was removed from the mausoleum, the poet, Yevgeny Yevtushenko, warned Russians that the ghost of Stalin was not yet laid to rest.

I dream
> That a telephone has been placed in the coffin.
Stalin sends instructions
> To Enver Hoxha.
Where else does the line from the coffin run.

No – Stalin has not given up.
> He considers death remediable.
We rooted him
> Out of the Mausoleum.
But how to root Stalin
> Out of Stalin's heir?
Some of the heirs snip roses in retirement
And secretly consider
> That retirement temporary.
Others
> Even condemn Stalin from the platform,
But themselves
> At night
> Pine for the old days,
As long as Stalin's heirs exist on earth
It will seem to me
> That Stalin is still in the Mausoleum.

Enver Hoxha (1908-1985): Albanian Communist leader and admirer of Stalin, who broke with the USSR over destalinization. Close ally of China 1960-76.

Stalin's Heirs by Yevgeny Yevtushenko, published in *Pravda*, 1962.

5 KHRUSHCHEV'S RUSSIA 1957-64

Among the nations gaining independence in this period were nearly all the former French, British and Belgian African colonies, including Algeria, Ghana and Nigeria, and many in the West Indies.

Source A
From a speech made by Khrushchev at the 22nd Party Congress, October 1961.

Source B
Tables compiled for *Purnell's History of the 20th Century* from figures published by the United States Census Bureau, 1966, and the official Soviet statistical collection, *Narodnoye Khozyaistvo SSSR* (The National Economy of the USSR) 1955 and 1966.

Consumption in the USSR as a percentage of consumption in the USA, 1955-66.

Introduction

By the late 1950s, the Soviet state was changing. Greater contact with the outside world had raised people's aspirations for a higher standard of living and more cultural freedom. The proliferation of nuclear weapons and the emergence of new nations in Africa and Asia had made the world outside a more complicated and dangerous place. How to cope with these pressures without undermining Soviet security or Party control was Khrushchev's dilemma.

Economic Experiments

In the coming decade, the Soviet Union, in creating the material and technical basis of Communism, will surpass the strongest and richest capitalist country, the USA, and by 1970 everyone will be in easy circumstances . . . there will be an abundance of material benefits for the whole population . . . output of foodstuffs, clothing, footwear, cars and other consumer goods will be increased to meet the growing demand in full . . . every family will have a comfortable flat conforming to the requirements of hygiene and cultured living . . . and between 1970 and 1980 the Soviet Union will come close to a state where it can introduce the principle of distribution according to need . . . .

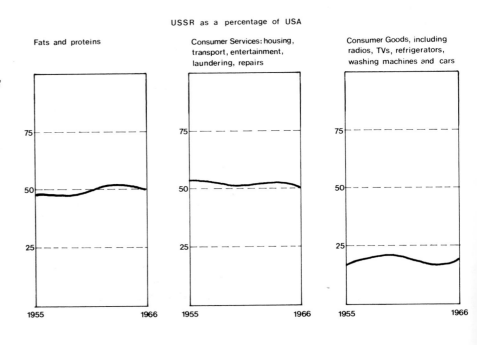

USSR as a percentage of USA

Fats and proteins | Consumer Services: housing, transport, entertainment, laundering, repairs | Consumer Goods, including radios, TVs, refrigerators, washing machines and cars

Source C
As for Source B.

Ownership of Household Consumer Goods in USA and USSR
(number per 1000 of population)

	USSR 1955	USSR 1966	USA 1966
Motor cars	2	5	398
TV sets	4	82	376
Refrigerators	4	40	293
Washing machines	1	77	259

???

1 How does Khrushchev foresee the future of the Soviet economy? Why does he think that such progress is so important for the future of Communism?

2 Do the figures in Source C make it look as if his dream is likely to come true?

3 What reasons might there have been for the inability of the Soviet economy to live up to Khrushchev's promises?

Malenkov in a speech on 8 August 1953 and Khrushchev in his speech of 13 September. Both admitted that the official production figures for 1952 had been grossly exaggerated.

Khrushchev had a genuine interest in agriculture and often visited collective farms to discuss farming methods with the locals. Historians have argued that his great weakness was a tendency to latch on to a new idea with great enthusiasm and to push it through without thinking out all the implications and not listening to the advice of experts like agronomists. The Virgin Lands scheme was an example of this.

Khrushchev staked his reputation on a dramatic rise in the Soviet standard of living. Shortly after Stalin's death both he and Malenkov had admitted publicly that agricultural output was being crippled by lack of investment and industry stifled by over-centralization. The years between 1957 and 1964 were marked by experiments to find solutions to these shortcomings. To reduce over-centralization, the USSR was divided in 1957 into 100 regions called *sovnarkhozi*, each of which was responsible for planning its own industrial development under the overall supervision of Moscow. Military spending was cut and more money invested in factories producing consumer goods and 'modern' products like fertilizers and chemicals. Investment in agriculture was quadrupled and included a rural electrification programme. Collective farmers were given a better deal, including much higher prices for their quotas. As in industry, more scope was given to each area to do its own planning and the Machine Tractor Stations were abolished. Under the Virgin Lands scheme, begun in 1954, a vast, semi-desert area of Southern Siberia and Kazakstan was ploughed up and irrigated, with the aim of transforming it into the USSR's main grain-growing area. The sight of thousands of tractors and harvesters strung out across the vast new fields became a regular feature of Soviet newsreels.

There is no question that under Khrushchev the standard of living rose for ordinary Russians. A crash building programme almost doubled the nation's housing stock. Everyday goods like shoes and woollen clothing became more plentiful, as did consumer goods like radios, television sets and refrigerators. There were large increases in the numbers of doctors, hospital beds and students in higher education. In many Soviet schools the pupil–teacher ratio was better than in Britain or the USA. Agricultural production rose by 56 per cent between 1954 and 1960, and the grain harvest of 1962 was a record 140 million tons. The variety of foods available in shops increased. Stalin's draconian labour laws were scrapped. By 1964 the average working day had been reduced to seven hours, with six hours on Saturday. All workers were guaranteed employment.

But as the statistics above show, achievements still fell far short of promises. Decentralization led to corruption and inefficiency, as local officials selfishly allocated scarce resources for their own region. In 1962 the number of

By the early 1960s, two-thirds of the USSR's milk, meat and potatoes, half its vegetables and nine-tenths of its eggs came from private plots.

The soil of the Virgin lands was fragile and needed to be looked after with frequent fallow periods and crop rotation. Khrushchev was too impatient to bother with all this and the price was paid in 1963.

Best-known of these economists was Abel Aganbegyan, then director of the Novosibirsk Institute of Economics. For his later career, see chapter 8.

Sputnik came as a great shock to the Americans, who had tended to regard Soviet technology as crude and backward. Gagarin's flight provoked President Kennedy into launching the US Apollo programme to put a man on the moon. This was achieved in July 1969. The space race had begun.

regional planning boards was halved and they were abolished altogether after Khrushchev's downfall. The armed forces chiefs obstructed defence cuts, and the soaring cost of the space and missile programme diverted investment from consumer goods. The full-employment policy made it difficult to sack workers, who had no incentive to take a pride in their work. Absenteeism and drunkenness were common. The greatest disappointment, however, was in agriculture. Growth slowed down in the early 1960s. For reasons that mystified Khrushchev, private plots were more productive than collective farms, leading him to complain that capitalist cows bred while socialist ones did not. And in the long run the Virgin Lands scheme failed, as overfarming led to erosion and dust bowls. In 1963 the grain harvest fell to 110 tons and the USSR was forced to buy wheat from the USA.

Some of the Soviet economists, whom Khrushchev consulted, dared to suggest that the remedy lay with a dose of Western-style free enterprise. If factories were judged by profitability rather than output, this would act as an incentive to both management and workforce, for wage-levels and job-security would depend on them turning out well-made goods that people would buy. Collective farmers would work harder if they were able to sell more of their produce themselves and keep the profits, instead of having to deliver most of it to the state at low prices. But in the early 1960s such a drastic break with the principles of the command economy was still inconceivable.

The Technological Giant

Centralized planning, though, made it possible for the USSR to make great strides in technology. A technology committee attached to the Council of Ministers oversaw all scientific research and gave it the money and men it needed. Priority was given to science in schools and universities. As a result the Soviet Union had quickly made good her lag in nuclear technology, and in the late Fifties took the lead in space research, launching the first-ever artificial satellite – Sputnik – in 1957. In April 1961 Yuri Gagarin became the first man in space, in 1963 Valentina Tereshkova the first woman.

The first nation in space. Premier Khrushchev arm-in-arm with Cosmonauts Valentina Tereshkova (the first woman in space) and Valerie Bykovski, at a reception in the Kremlin in June 1963.

In his retirement Khrushchev, who was responsible for the expensive space programme, drew attention to a great irony of Soviet life, which also struck many visitors:

You have probably seen on more than one occasion how men and women are engaged in chipping ice off the pavement with crowbars . . . . Such a sight really makes one uncomfortable. So much has been done in our country to mechanize complicated production processes . . . and the first artificial earth satellites have been developed, but as for replacing the crowbar and the shovel with a machine – we have not got around to that. We pay too little attention to such matters and regard them as trivial. But is this trivial? No, it is 'trivial matters' like this that constitute the work of many people.

From Khrushchev Remembers, 1971.

The Limits of Freedom

With the disappearance of Stalin's terror, demands for more cultural and political freedom sprung up. In her memoirs, written in 1963, Stalin's daughter, Svetlana, wrote of the great hunger among her contemporaries, who had been walled off for so long from the rest of the world, for new ideas and free discussion. The young poets Yevtushenko and Voznesensky, who wrote openly about the spirit of post-Stalinist Russia, drew huge audiences when they gave public readings. The literary magazine *Novy Mir* ('New World'), edited by Alexander Tvardovsky, printed stories and poems that would have been condemned in Stalin's day. Many writers dug out manuscripts that they had written years before and hidden away in desk drawers, hoping they could now be published. The most famous example of this was Boris Pasternak's *Dr Zhivago*, which, however, never actually appeared in the USSR.

At first, hopes for a real cultural thaw ran high, especially in 1962 when Khrushchev personally authorized the publication of *One Day in the Life of Ivan Denisovitch* – a description of daily life in a Stalinist camp by the then-unknown school teacher, Alexander Solzhenitsyn, which became a best-seller.

Svetlana Alliluyeva, *Twenty Letters to a Friend*. This was never published in the USSR; only in the West, after the author's defection in 1966.

The theme of *Dr Zhivago* was the disillusion of Russian intellectuals with the brutality of the 1917 revolution. Pasternak first offered the novel to *Novy Mir* in 1956, who turned it down (presumably because it was too radical). It was then published in Italy in 1957. It won its author the Nobel Prize for Literature in 1958, which he was forced by the Soviet authorities to turn down.

Other outspoken works published in 1962 were Yuri Bondarev's *Silence* (another account of Stalin's terror), Yevtushenko's *Babi Yar*, which revealed Soviet anti-semitism and the poem *Stalin's Heirs*.

A man of the people. Khrushchev joins in a local folk dance during a visit to Yugoslavia in August 1963.

Source A

Solzhenitsyn, *The Gulag Archipelago*, vol. 3 (1978). The author is describing the reaction to *One Day in the Life of Ivan Denisovitch*.

Zek: Russian prison slang for a prisoner.

Source B

From a speech by Khrushchev to Moscow metal-workers, published in *Pravda*, 26 April, 1963.

Only members of the Writers Union could publish legally, and expulsion deprived a writer of his livelihood. Another method of controlling a writer was to find a doctor who would certify the accused was mentally ill. They could then be incarcerated against their will and kept drugged, as happened to Valery Tarsis who wrote a fictionalized memoir of the 1945-53 period entitled *Ward 7*. This method was only rarely used under Khrushchev but more frequently in the late Sixties and in the Seventies.

I had this good fortune: to thrust the first handful of truth through the open jaws of the iron gates before they slammed shut again.

Like matter enveloped by antimatter, it exploded instantaneously.

When former *zeks* started reading it, a single groan broke from all those thousands – a groan of joy and pain. Letters started pouring in.

I treasure those letters. Only rarely do our fellow countrymen have a chance to speak their minds on matters of public concern . . . yet now they believed that the era of truth was really beginning, that at last it was possible to speak and write boldly.

Some creative intellectuals have drawn the wrong conclusions from the party's efforts to overcome the injurious consequences of the Stalin cult. They failed to understand that struggle against the cult does not mean weakening authority. Some have even begun to assert that the time has come when everyone can determine his own conduct without considering the interests of society and the state. This is nothing but an anarchist idea, hostile to Marxism-Leninism.

? ?

1 What can we gather from Sources A and B about the immediate effects of the publication of *One Day in the Life of Ivan Denisovitch*?

2 Why did this frighten the Party leaders?

3 Khrushchev's speech was a warning of what was to come? What do you think that was?

The public reaction to *One Day in the Life of Ivan Denisovitch* taught the Party that a little freedom could be a dangerous thing and during 1963 the censorship was tightened again. Although there was no return to the total orthodoxy and isolation of Stalin's time and writers who steered clear of politics found it easier to publish, hopes of a real thaw were dashed. In December the USSR's first-ever exhibition of abstract art was closed down by Khrushchev after only a few days. The pictures looked, he said, as if they had been painted with 'the tail of a donkey'. New means were found to keep writers who defied censorship under control, such as expulsion from the Writers' Union or compulsory commitment to a psychiatric hospital. For the average citizen, who minded his own business and kept out of politics, the terror and unpredictability of the Stalin years were over, but for the creative artist life remained precarious. Nothing as daring as *Ivan Denisovitch* was to be published in Russia for many years to come.

The USSR and the World

The thaw continued until 1960. In 1959 Khrushchev made the first-ever visit by a Soviet leader to the United States. A summit meeting was planned for the spring of 1960, to be held in Paris. No concessions were made, though, on the vital issues of disarmament and Berlin and no secret was made of the belief that co-existence was not friendship, but only a means of averting a devastating war long enough for the world to see for itself the superiority of the Communist way of life. It did not end the arms race, nor rivalry with the USA for the hearts and minds of the peoples of the world. Many Western politicians found this policy hard to fathom and saw Khrushchev as unpredictable and inconsistent, while it is clear from what happened later that some of his Politburo colleagues thought him too soft on the West.

Emerging Third World nations of whatever political colour, including Egypt, Ghana, India and Indonesia, were wooed with lavish economic aid. The USSR financed the building of the Aswan Dam in Egypt, which the USA had refused to do, so that it received:

> . . . the priceless prize of the Egyptian people's trust and gratitude. And not just the trust of the Egyptian people, but the trust of all Arabs. And not just the trust of all Arabs, but of all other undeveloped countries, especially in Africa.

In the Congolese civil war 1960-4, the USSR backed the government in Leopoldville against the breakaway province of Katanga. The Arab states were given military aid in their quarrel against the USA's ally, Israel. Thousands of African students came to Moscow to study at the Lumumba University at the Soviet government's expense.

Khrushchev, who loved to travel, was a frequent guest in the capitals of Asia and the Middle East.

In 1960 the thaw ended. It is still not entirely clear why. Khrushchev may have been under pressure from hard-line colleagues in the Politburo, who thought he was too soft on the West, or he may have seen election year in the USA as a chance to make easy gains at the USA's expense. In May an American U2 spy plane was shot down deep inside Soviet territory. When Eisenhower refused to apologize Khrushchev stormed out of the Paris Summit. In August 1961 the Berlin Wall was put up to cut off all access between East and West Berlin, and to stop refugees escaping to the west. When President Castro of Cuba, the USA's close neighbour, turned to the Soviet Union for economic aid in 1960, the price asked by Khrushchev was permission to set up long-range nuclear missiles on Cuban soil, which would tip the strategic balance in the USSR's favour. If he expected no American retaliation, he miscalculated, for Kennedy called his bluff with a naval blockade. Soviet ships bringing parts for the bases would have to turn back or risk confrontation with the US navy. For six days the world stood on the brink of a major war. Of the debates that went on behind the closed doors of the Politburo we have no direct evidence, but on Friday 26 October two letters from Moscow arrived in Washington within hours of each other.

From *Khrushchev Remembers*, p. 403.

Leopoldville: now Kinshasa.

Patrice Lumumba (1925-61): first Prime Minister of the independent Congo 1960-1, whose cause in the Congolese civil war (1960-4) was supported by the USSR. He was murdered by Katanganese troops in 1961.

In the November 1960 Presidential election, the inexperienced 43-year-old John F. Kennedy became the youngest ever US President.

Fidel Castro had come to power in 1959 by overthrowing the US-backed dictator, Batista. When he nationalized all businesses in Cuba, including American-owned sugar firms, the USA retaliated by boycotting Cuban sugar and cutting off the island's oil supply, thereby ruining the economy.

Cuba is only 90 miles (145 km) from Florida. The Soviet missiles were capable of hitting most of the major cities of North and South America. It was estimated that within a few minutes of their being fired 80 million Americans would be dead.

Amid rising tensions, Khrushchev and Kennedy meet in Vienna for a superpower summit, 3 June 1961.

Source A
Letter signed by Khrushchev as Chairman of the Council of Ministers that arrived in Washington DC at 6 pm on Friday, 26 October 1962.

If indeed war should break out, then it would not be in our power to stop it, for such is the logic of war. I have participated in two wars and know that war ends when it has rolled through cities and villages, everywhere sowing death and destruction . . . . We do not want this . . . only lunatics and suicides, who themselves want to perish and to destroy the whole world before they die, could do this . . . . If assurances were given that the President of the United States would not attack Cuba and the blockade be lifted, then the question of the removal or the destruction of the missile sites on Cuba would then be an entirely different question.

Your rockets are stationed in Britain and in Italy and pointed at us. Your rockets are stationed in Turkey.

You are worried over Cuba. You say it worries you because it lies at a distance of ninety miles [145 km] across the sea from the shores of the United States. However, Turkey lies next to us . . . . Do you believe that you have the right to demand security for your country and the removal of such weapons that you qualify as offensive, while not recognizing this right for us?

This is why I make this proposal: We agree to remove those weapons from Cuba . . . and to state this commitment in the United Nations. Your representatives will make a statement to the effect that the United States, on its part, bearing in mind the anxiety and concern of the Soviet state, will evacuate its analogous weapons from Turkey.

Source B
From a letter, also signed by Khrushchev, which arrived in Washington early in the morning of Saturday, 27 October 1962.

? ?

1 What is the difference in the tone of the two letters and the offers they make?

2 What clues about what was going on behind the scenes in the Politburo can be gleaned from the fact that these two letters were sent so close together?

3 Later on the Saturday, the Soviet ships turned back. Soon after, the missiles were withdrawn, without a similar commitment by the USA over the NATO missiles in Turkey. Why do you think this happened?

It was probably Khrushchev himself, aware that he had brought the world to the verge of war, who insisted on the climb-down over Cuba, against the hard-liners in the Kremlin, who had made him write the second, more aggressive letter. It was a humiliation for the USSR but also a statesman-like decision, that may have saved the peace. Over the next 12 months, the two leaders, who had emerged from the crisis with mutual respect for each other, worked on ways to avert future confrontations. A new thaw was born. In August 1963 the Hot Line, a direct telex link between the Kremlin and the White House, was set up so that the two leaders could talk to each other directly and avoid war by misunderstanding. In July the Partial Test Ban Treaty was signed.

This outlawed the testing of nuclear weapons above ground. It was signed by the USSR, USA and Britain, but not by China and France, two new nuclear powers.

Also known as the Sino-Soviet split.

The Quarrel with China

In the early 1960s the world was taken by surprise when a bitter quarrel between the USSR and China became public, although it is now clear that tensions had been building up for many years. The causes were economic, strategic and racial as well as ideological. The Chinese condemned peaceful co-existence as a surrender to capitalism, the Russians accused the Chinese (who had stuck to the Stalinist line of the inevitability of war between East and West) of irresponsible war-mongering. While Soviet propaganda criticized the Chinese system of rural communism as 'un-Marxist', China claimed that the USSR had betrayed Communism by running after capitalist living standards. Beneath this lay rivalry for the leadership of the Communist world and centuries of mutual distrust. In the nineteenth century, Tsarist Russia had taken advantage of China's weakness to annex territory along the 5500-mile (9000km) frontier they shared. Both before and after the revolution, China's teeming population had worried her neighbour. Even when they were allies, the Soviet Union had refused to share her atomic secrets.

This did not stop China exploding her own atomic bomb in 1964.

As the quarrel erupted in 1960, the USSR withdrew all aid, throwing

Shifting allegiances . . . Mao Zedong with Joseph Stalin (1950), with Nikita Khrushchev (1957) and with US President Richard Nixon (1972).

China's economy into disarray. Soviet technicians living in China were abruptly recalled. The unity of the Communist world was shattered and the USSR no longer its undisputed leader. When Khrushchev fell from power in 1964 there was no sign of the dispute abating.

Mikhail Suslov (1902-1982): Politburo member from 1955, he was responsible for ideology and an opponent of experiments with freer speech. Remained influential in Soviet politics until his death.

At a meeting of the General Assembly of the United Nations in 1960, for example, he had taken off his shoe and banged it on the table in protest at what was being said.

An article in *Pravda* on 17 October 1964, which did not mention Khrushchev by name, condemned 'bragging, phrasemongering and bossiness' as unworthy of Communist leaders. This is one of the clearest clues we have to the roots of Khrushchev's unpopularity in the party by 1964.

M. Franklin, *Khrushchev* (Penguin, 1966).

Khrushchev's Fall

By 1964 Khrushchev had made many enemies both in the Politburo and the lower ranks of the party, which had put him in power in 1957. Among the reasons for this were the humiliation over Cuba, the dangerous quarrel with China and the failure of the Virgin Lands scheme, on which he had staked his reputation. He had alienated the army by his cuts in the military budget. Some Politburo members like Suslov were worried that liberalization in the arts had gone too far and threatened the security of the state. Others thought his economic experiments 'hare-brained'. Khrushchev's extrovert and boisterous behaviour, especially on trips abroad, was seen as undignified. He was consulting his colleagues less and less and becoming increasingly dictatorial. He gave jobs to his family and friends, including his son-in-law, who became editor of the important newspaper *Izvestiya*.

In October, while he was on holiday by the Black Sea, his enemies struck. As in 1957, a Central Committee meeting was called and Khrushchev ordered to appear before it. This time, however, the vote went against him and he was sacked, although the official reason was given out as retirement on the grounds of ill-health. He was allowed to retire into obscurity on a state pension and live out his life in peace – a beneficiary of his own humanization of Soviet political life. His place was taken by the collective leadership of Leonid Brezhnev as party secretary and Alexei Kosygin as Chairman of the Council of Ministers.

Conclusion

The Soviet state that Khrushchev left behind was a one-party dictatorship. Its citizens had few guaranteed civil liberties. The standard of living remained comparatively low and agriculture underproductive. In spite of this, the USSR had come a long way since the hardships and fear of Stalin's last years, and for everyone the world now seemed a safer place. Khrushchev, as his biographer, Mark Franklin, wrote of him in 1966, had 'left his country a better place than he found it, both in the eyes of the majority of his own people, and of the world.'

Disgraced but alive. Khrushchev photographed in retirement at his country home in 1967, three years after he was forced to step down as Premier.

6 THE YEARS OF STAGNATION: THE USSR AT HOME 1964~85

The term for rule by old men is gerontocracy. A good example is Andrei Gromyko, who was Foreign Minister from 1957 to 1985.

Alexei Kosygin (1904-1980): Economic administrator, who had been a member of the Politburo since 1960. Joined opposition to Khrushchev in 1964, possibly on the grounds that some of his economic experiments were too badly thought out.

By 1982 nine out of ten Soviet homes had a television set (about a third of them in colour) and a refrigerator. The gradual improvement in diet since 1945 (more protein and less bread and potato) has led to an increase of 2.8 inches (7.1 cm) in the average height of Soviet women over the last 30 years.

In 1987 only 45 out of 1000 Soviet citizens owned a car. Servicing and parts were so expensive that it cost 875 roubles a year to run one, about a third of the average income. Automatic washing machines were rare.

Introduction

The members of the Politburo that ousted Khrushchev hung on to power for the next 20 years. By 1982 their average age was 70. These men, often of humble origin, had made good careers in the Party and their view of the world had been forged during World War II. Their aim was to avoid any risks that might endanger Party control over the state and their own position in it, or that would weaken Soviet security abroad. It is hardly surprising, therefore, that there were few new ideas and little progress was made towards solving the USSR's serious economic and social problems. All talk of the coming of the perfect communist society and the withering away of the state by 1980 was dropped.

For a decade Brezhnev and Kosygin shared power. By the mid-1970s, however, General Secretary Brezhnev, like his predecessors, had come out on top. He had himself promoted to the rank of Marshal of the Soviet Union and commander-in-chief of the armed forces. In 1977 he became President as well, although this was largely a ceremonial role. When Kosygin died in 1980, Brezhnev's own supporter, Nikolai Tikhonov, became Chairman of the Council of Ministers. When Brezhnev himself finally died in 1982, he was succeeded by the elderly Yuri Andropov, who himself died in February 1984, and then by Konstantin Chernenko, who was ill for most of his 13 months in power.

Economic Stagnation

In some ways, the Soviet economy performed impressively. By 1975 she produced more steel, oil and cement than the USA and in total output ranked second in the world. Surpluses from the huge Siberian natural gas field discovered in 1965 were exported via a pipeline to Western Europe. The unemployment and inflation that dogged Western economies in the mid-Seventies largely passed the USSR by. There were further advances in space technology, including the first permanent orbiting space station – Salyut I – launched in 1971. Living standards, as measured by the ownership of consumer goods, went on rising, and people were better fed. Rural life improved as more schools and roads were built and prices paid by the state for produce went up. By 1976 most farm labourers were paid a regular wage and the average income was only about 10 per cent less than that of an unskilled factory worker.

Nevertheless, all was far from well. Labour-saving devices and cars remained expensive and hard to get, making daily life far harder than in the West. Living space was cramped, the typical family apartment in a city

In an interview in 1985 with a BBC film crew for the programme *Comrades*, first shown on British TV in 1986, the world famous Soviet eye surgeon, Fyodorov, complained that Soviet-made microscopes were too crude and imprecise for his delicate work and that he had to use microscopes imported from East Germany and the West.

Most Russians were in the habit of carrying with them at all times an *avoska* or 'on the off-chance' string bag, in case they unexpectedly came across a shop selling hard-to-find goods.

For details on defence spending 1964-85, see chapter 7.

Quoted in *The Waking Giant, The Soviet Union under Gorbachev* by Martin Walker (Abacus, 1987).

A technological superpower. Ballistic missiles form the centrepiece of the 51st Anniversary October Revolution Parade in 1968.

consisting of two or three rooms plus a bathroom. Mysterious shortages of essential goods like light bulbs or toilet paper were common. The service sector was so neglected that it was difficult to get things like plumbing or household appliances repaired. The USSR lagged behind the West in automation, computers and other aspects of new technology. The official Soviet yearbook for 1973 rated Soviet agriculture as one quarter as efficient as that of America. Supplies of fruit, vegetables and meat were often erratic, and queuing for scarce foodstuffs was a normal part of daily life. In 1972, 1975, 1976 and 1982 the harvest was so poor that grain had to be brought from abroad again, although the weather was partly to blame, especially in 1972. By the early 1980s the whole economy was on the decline, and the growth rate, even for heavy industry, had slowed down. The Soviet Union, it was being said, was a first-rate power resting on a Third-World economy. To these problems the elderly men in the Kremlin had no answer and things were allowed to drift.

The source of the problem was not so different from in Khrushchev's day. Innovation was discouraged by bureaucracy. High defence spending in the 1970s and the nuclear arms race diverted resources away from civilian industries. The centralized planning system was too inflexible to adapt easily to the manufacture of consumer goods, for the planners often had little idea what people actually wanted to buy but the state monopoly meant that dissatisfied consumers could not take their money elsewhere. Work discipline remained lax. Bonuses were paid so long as the annual target was met, so no one cared much about workmanship or quality and Soviet goods were often shoddy. A worker in a Lithuanian television factory told *Guardian* correspondent, Martin Walker, in 1984:

We never use a screwdriver in the last week. We hammer the screws in. We slam solder on to the connections, cannibalize parts from other TVs if we have run out of the right ones, use glue or hammers to fix switches that were never meant for that model. And all the time management is pressing us to work faster, to make the target so that we can all get our bonuses.

To combat the difficulties of daily life, an unofficial 'black economy' sprang up. Workers with skills would 'moonlight' by doing repair jobs in their spare time, often with tools lifted from their workplace. Scarce articles like footwear were made at home with raw materials pilfered from state supplies and sold on the black market. Many skilled people including doctors sold their services in return for a bribe or *blat* in the shape of a hard-to-get consumer item. Anyone who got hold of foreign goods like Japanese cameras or Scotch whiskey was sure of being able to sell them privately at a huge profit. While fruit and vegetables were short in state shops, every town had its *kolkhoz* or collective farm market, where a much greater variety of produce, grown on private plots, could be bought, although prices were three to four times as high. Moonlighters or *shabashniki* and black marketeers often bribed local party officials to overlook their illegal activities. A notorious example of corruption was uncovered in Georgia in 1972, in which the wife of the Party Secretary there was arrested for taking bribes from two brothers, who ran a network of illegal workshops making clothes for the black market.

Getting to the Top

The only way to the top in Soviet politics was through the Communist Party hierarchy, as the party controlled every appointment of any importance in all walks of life, including the top jobs in the media, industry and the universities. An ambitious young person started by joining the bottom rung of the Party at their college or workplace. If he (it usually was a *he*) was lucky, he moved up the hierarchy by impressing his superiors, who recommended them for vacancies as they occurred. Even though all party posts were theoretically elective, this system of patronage extended right up into the Central Committee and the Politburo. Brezhnev, for example, attracted the attention of Ukrainian Party Secretary Khrushchev during the war years, when he was a young political officer with the Red Army there. It was Khrushchev who opened the way for his rapid rise in the 1950s and brought him into the Politburo in 1957. As Party Secretary Brezhnev himself gave many jobs to colleagues he had worked with in the Ukraine. They were nicknamed the Dnieper Mafia after the river there.

Top party officials did fall from power, as Khrushchev's experience showed, and were sometimes sacked for incompetence or corruption. But after 1964 this old boys' network (as it would be called in the West) proved very resistent to change. Its members protected each other and shut out outsiders. This was why Brezhnev managed to hold on to office until he died and why the Politburo chose elderly, ailing men, who could be guaranteed not to rock the boat, as his successors.

A successful party career guaranteed a higher than average standard of living. Top party members were able to shop at special stores for goods not available elsewhere, had comfortable flats and dachas (country houses) and were able to push their children into the best schools and universities.

Soviet Society

Ever since the 1930s education had been seen as a key to economic growth, and by 1980 the USSR was a highly-educated society. In 1979 70.5 per cent of 18-year-olds completed secondary school education and over a quarter of these went on to some form of higher education. In spite of censorship, Soviet citizens were probably much better informed about the outside world than most Westerners assumed. Many spoke a foreign language and listened to foreign stations on their radios. Soviet scientists and scholars attended international conferences and a growing number of foreign tourists visited the

Unlike the black market in consumer goods, Kolkhoz markets were not illegal.

Detailed information about the inner workings of the Soviet system were revealed to the West by Mikhail Voslensky, a Moscow professor who defected in 1972.

Political officer: Communist party member who was attached to a unit of the armed forces to ensure the political loyalty of the soldiers. This system went back to the early days of the Red Army in 1918, when they were called political commissars.

One of the first things that the Western press noticed about Raisa Gorbachev, wife of the new Party Secretary in 1985, was how elegantly she dressed (up to then Kremlin wives had been rather dowdy). This was only possible for someone who had access to special shops and foreign goods.

The opportunity for working people, who missed out on higher education in their youth, to study for degrees part-time in the evenings is far greater than in most Western countries and many people take advantage of this. One distinctive feature of the Soviet education system at all levels are the political courses such as Dialectical Materialism or scientific atheism, which all students have to take in addition to their chosen subjects.

A rising standard of living. Houses under construction in Barnayl Tcheriomushki, 1965.

What they replaced. Slum dwellings like these could still be found away from the main thoroughfares of Moscow in the early sixties.

Equality for women was one of the early aims of the revolution in 1917. Lenin regarded housework as no fit work for an intelligent adult of either sex.

In 1986 Alexandra Biryukova was appointed as one of the 15 Central Committee secretaries, who oversee all Party work. She was the first woman to hold this post.

USSR. In spite of official disapproval, young Russians learned about Western pop culture and even developed an unofficial protest culture of their own, exemplified by the poet and singer, Vladimir Vysotsky. Although he was never allowed to sing on radio or television, his songs about the seamier side of Soviet life spread by word of mouth across the country. Whatever the wishes of the leadership, it was impossible to recreate the closed society of Stalin's day.

Soviet women experienced many problems that would be familiar to their Western counterparts, often, though, to a greater degree. The idea that women should contribute to society was more deeply engrained than in the West. According to the 1970 census, 70 per cent of women had full-time jobs outside the home. Few Russian women, though, reached the very top. Since 1945 only one woman had held a top political post – Katerina Furtseva, who was a Politburo member and Minister of Culture from 1957 to 1960. For all working women, the 'double load' was a serious problem.

Source A

From a short story *One Week Like Any Other* by Natalya Baranskaya, published in *Novy Mir* in 1969. In this extract the heroine, Olga, a working mother of two, is filling in an official questionnaire asking women how they use their leisure time.

Source B

From a letter published in *Moscow News*, March 1980.

Source C

Statistics published by the Soviet Sociological Institute in 1981.

'Akh, leisure, leisure', she mused. 'It's rather an awkward word . . . . It's something alien – leisure. Personally, I'm attracted to sports – to running. I run here. I run there. With bundles of shopping in each arm. I run up. I run down. Into the tram, into the bus, into the subway and out. We don't have any stores in our district. We have been living there more than a year, but they are still not built.'

One morning I went out for milk with my baby in a pram. In our town milk is sold in churns on the street. There was a queue. I asked them to let me have milk for my baby without having to wait. Everyone called out, 'Why don't you get up earlier?' Have they forgotten how little sleep you get when you have a baby? I went away without the milk.

Family Size in the USSR

	Average number of children in family		
	1959	1970	1979
Russian Republic	1.6	1.5	1.3
Ukraine	1.5	1.4	1.3
Latvia and Estonia	1.2	1.2	1.1
Tadzhikistan	2.7	3.4	3.7
Uzbekistan	2.6	3.4	3.7
Turkmenia	2.5	3.2	3.5

Divorce rate in USSR

Divorces per 1000 marriages	
1965	1979
103	340

? ?

1 What is the 'double load'? What clues are given in Sources A and B to explain why it is a particular problem for women in the USSR?

2 What other difficulties might they encounter in their daily lives?

3 What might the connection be between the evidence in Sources A and B and the Statistics in Source C? Why should the trends outlined there worry the government?

The low birth rate in the European republics was regarded as a serious problem, as the populations there were actually falling, whereas those in Muslim Soviet Central Asia were rising fast and it was estimated that of those under 18 years of age in the USSR 40 per cent would come from here by the year 2000. This worried Party members, who were never sure how firmly Communism had really taken root in Muslim areas. But incentives like higher family allowances or longer paid maternity leave did little to persuade Russian women to have more children. In the western half of the USSR the one-child family had become the norm.

Other social problems included antisocial behaviour among the young, and widespread alcoholism. Between 1970 and 1980 sales of alcohol, especially

Almost half the divorce cases in Soviet courts cite the husband's drunkenness as the main grounds.

According to Marxist theory, religion and national distinctions should disappear as a country moves towards socialism. This has shown no sign of happening in the USSR.

Brezhnev's Politburo consisted almost entirely of Russians and Ukrainians, as did 83% of the Central Committee and most of the top army officers. These two nationalities make up slightly less than 70% of the population.

A *refusnik*, Anatoly Shcharansky, who spent ten years in prison has published his prison memoirs called *Speak No Evil*. They were serialized in *The Sunday Times* on 15 and 22 May.

vodka, rose by 77 per cent. The effect on family life and efficiency at work was so great that the matter was frequently discussed openly in the press. As the Soviet media became more frank after 1985 (see chapter 8), it was admitted that many young Russians were so at odds with Soviet society that they had turned to drugs or Western cults like punk.

The USSR was a multinational state, in which cultural differences and local nationalism remained strong. In the 1970s plans to make Russian the official 'first' language of the whole country had to be abandoned when violent protests broke out in Georgia and Estonia. The stranglehold of the Russians over political power in Moscow caused much resentment. Islam remained strong in the Central Asian republics. Jewish consciousness also increased from the mid-1960s. Many who applied to emigrate to Israel were refused permission. Those who protested against the ban were nicknamed *refusniks* and some suffered periods of imprisonment.

New flats in Moscow, 1970s. All mod cons, though still small and primitive by western standards.

Street life in Ashkhalabad, Soviet Central Asia – a mingling of old and new. The USSR is a country of many races and cultures.

Dissent

Although there was no return to the wholesale terror of Stalin's day and a certain amount of grumbling about the hardships of daily life was reluctantly tolerated, no serious criticism of the Soviet system, past or present, was permitted. Awkward issues like the role of Stalin in Soviet history were simply ignored. In 1966 two young writers, Andrei Sinyavsky and Yuli Daniel, whose short stories satirizing Soviet life had been published in the West, were sentenced to seven and five years in a labour camp for spreading 'anti-Soviet propaganda'. Solzhenitsyn's two later novels, *Cancer Ward* and *The First Circle* were never published in the USSR. Public demonstrations, like the one in Moscow protesting against the invasion of Czechoslovakia in 1968, were quickly broken up by the police.

Frustrated by the stifling of the short-lived thaw of 1958-62, a handful of prominent intellectuals, among them the novelist Solzhenitsyn, the nuclear physicist Andrei Sakharov, the historian Roy Medvedev and his brother Zhores, a geneticist, began to voice protests against the lack of cultural and political freedom in Soviet life. As those who spoke out openly were usually swiftly silenced, these dissidents found ways around the censorship. Documents were typed out at home on carbon paper and copies passed round by hand. This was known as *samizdat* or 'self-publishing'. The best-known example was the *Chronicle of Current Events*, which began in 1968 and broadcast cases of human rights violations in the USSR. Manuscripts were given to foreign journalists to smuggle out of the country, and sometimes the contents were broadcast back to Soviet listeners by Western radio stations like *Voice of America*.

Examples of the sort of criticism reluctantly tolerated after 1964 are Sources A and B on page 39.

Cancer Ward (1968) was set in the period immediately after Stalin's death, *The First Circle* (1969) in a labour camp in the 1945-53 era.

For a first-hand account of some demonstrations and the fate of the demonstrators in the period 1968-76, see Andrei Almarik, *Notes of a Revolutionary* (1982).

Voice of America: a pro-Western radio station broadcasting out of West Germany.

Source A

From the speech made by Andrei Almarik during his trial in 1970 on charges of spreading anti-Soviet defamation in his book *Will the Soviet Union survive until 1984?*, which had been published abroad. The trial was held in secret, with only his wife and the judges present, but news of the speech was smuggled out. Almarik was sentenced to three and a half years in a labour camp.

It seems to me that now the main task of my country is to unburden itself of the heavy weight of the past, and for this, criticism is necessary above all, not glorification.

I think I am a better patriot than those who, loudly declaring their love for the motherland, by love for the motherland mean love for their own privileges.

Neither the witch hunt carried out by the regime, nor this trial arouses in me the slightest respect nor any fear. I understand that such trials are counted on to frighten many, and many will be frightened. But all the same, every free word spoken is a step towards the beginning of people's liberation from debasing fear and crushing tyranny. The process, having begun, will be irreversible.

Source B

From the first edition of *The Journal of Current Events*, April 1968.

Let the person from whom you received this paper know of the information available to you; he will pass it on to the person from whom he received his copy, and the process will be repeated. It would be unwise, however, to pursue the chain yourself, for in that way you might be taken for an informer.

? ?

1 Even though he is only one man against many, why does Almarik consider that it is so important to speak out?

2 What sort of 'information' does the extract in Source B refer to? What can we learn from it about the way such information was gathered and passed around in the USSR?

3 Which of the two ways of protesting shown above would be most effective in reaching most people and why?

Sakharov and his wife, Yelena Bonner, herself also a dissident, were exiled in 1980 to Gorky, a city 300 miles (559.2 km) from Moscow which was closed to foreigners. In 1983 Soviet psychiatrists were threatened with expulsion from the World Psychiatric Association for professional misconduct, because of the part some of them had played in diagnosing dissenters as mentally unbalanced. The Soviet doctors withdrew voluntarily before they could be thrown out.

One by one the dissenters were silenced. Some, like Almarik, were tried and imprisoned under vague charges. Others, like Solzhenitsyn, were expelled from the country or, like Sakharov, exiled to a remote part of the country, where they could be kept isolated from their friends. Compulsory confinement in mental hospitals was used more often. By the end of the Seventies the dissident movement had been all but broken up. It had drawn the world's attention towards Soviet affairs, but had changed little at home.

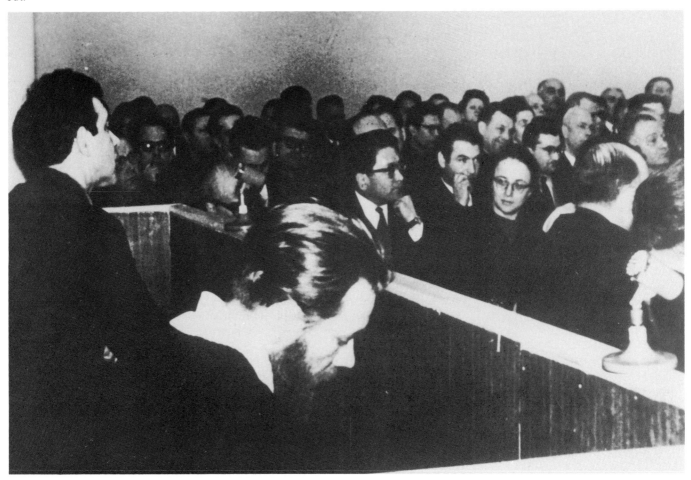

Andrei Sinyavsky (foreground) and Yuli Daniel (left) stand trial in 1966 for slandering the Soviet Union in books smuggled to the West.

Reports of Chernenko's speech appeared in all the main Moscow newspapers on 14 June 1983.

Conclusion

In June 1983 Chernenko, then in charge of culture and ideology, criticized Soviet film-makers for showing too much about the 'seamy' side of Soviet life like teenage crime, marital stress and drunkenness. They should concentrate instead on the positive values of communism and exposing the vices of capitalism. There can be no clearer illustration of the gap that had opened between Party propaganda, which painted the USSR in rosy colours, and the economic hardships and shabbiness of daily life. Unable to protest openly, people had grown cynical, took little interest in their work and despised politics. From what happened after 1985 it was apparent that the younger generation of communist leaders were aware of it too and were convinced that the USSR's survival as a super-power was threatened, unless it could once again harness the loyalty and enthusiasm of its people.

7 THE USSR AND THE WORLD 1964~85

Introduction

The change of leadership in 1964 did not bring about an immediate revision of Soviet foreign policy, as had happened after 1953. Until the late 1970s, co-existence and rivalry with the USA and the defence of Soviet security in Eastern Europe remained the cornerstones of the USSR's relations with the rest of the world.

Czechoslovakia in 1968

Another challenge to Soviet control of Eastern Europe arose in 1968, this time in Czechoslovakia, hitherto the most dependable of the satellite countries. With the enthusiastic support of the Czech people, the new party leader, Alexander Dubcek, brought in changes designed to create what he called socialism with a human face. Censorship disappeared and police powers curtailed. Plans were drawn up to reduce state control over industry and give employees a real say in how their factories were run. More contacts were opened with the West.

Aware of the Hungarian experience of 1956, Dubcek was careful to stress that he had no intention of allowing Czechoslovakia to become a multi-party state or to leave the Warsaw pact, and it was hoped that this time the Russians would not intervene. But on 21 August Soviet troops, supported by contingents from East Germany, Poland, Hungary and Bulgaria, invaded Czechoslovakia. Over the next six months the reforms of the Prague Spring were dismantled and a 'reliable' government led by Gustav Husak installed.

Dubcek replaced Antonin Novotny as party secretary in March 1968.

The installation of Husak was accompanied by a full-scale purge against anyone connected with the Prague Spring. Dubcek himself was forced into obscurity, ending up as a forestry inspector.

Source A
Two Thousand Words, written by the Czech scientist, Ludvik Vaculik and published 27 June 1968. Dubcek disassociated the CCP from it.

The reform movement has not yet brought us anything new . . . . The new ideas of this Spring have not prevailed because of their truth but because, after twenty years, the old leadership was tired and collapsed . . . . But our opponents are not yet defeated and may yet take their revenge. There is no reason yet for national jubilation, only for a new hope.

We address you at this moment of hope, which is, however, being threatened all the time . . . only we, the people, can complete our intention of humanizing this regime . . . let us therefore keep a close watch on events, let us understand them and respond to them. Let us give up the impossible demand that someone higher up should always hand down the only explanation . . . . Everyone will have to draw his own conclusion, on his own responsibility . . . .

In the coming days we have to take the initiative and make our own decisions.

Prague, Czechoslovakia, 1968. Soviet tanks drive demonstrators off the streets.

Source B

From an article in *Pravda*, 12 September 1968. The principle stated here soon became nicknamed 'The Brezhnev Doctrine'.

The right of every nation to take its own road to socialism must be limited by the duty of each nation not to damage either socialism in their own country nor the fundamental interests of the other socialist countries, nor the worldwide workers' movement, which is waging a struggle for socialism .... The Soviet Union and other socialist states, in fulfilling their internationalist duty to the fraternal peoples of Czechoslovakia, had to act and did act in resolute opposition to the anti-socialist forces in Czechoslovakia.

? ?

1 On what grounds does Source A argue that the Czechoslovak people must take events into their own hands? Why do you think that Dubcek dissociated himself from it?

2 How might the Kremlin react to such a document and how might it colour their view of what was going on inside Czechoslovakia? Are your conclusions backed up by the content of Source B?

3 How do Sources A and B together help to explain the Soviet decision to invade in August?

Founded in August 1980 as a result of the strikes in the Lenin Shipyard in Gdansk, which forced the resignation of Party Secretary Gierek. Its best-known leader is Lech Walesa.

Another challenge to the USSR's control over Eastern Europe occurred in Poland in 1980-81 with the rise of the free trade union, Solidarity, which challenged the Communist Party's monopoly of power. This time the Russians did not intervene so quickly or so directly, but in December 1981 (16 months after the crisis began) pressurized the Polish leader, General Jaruzelski, into declaring martial law and restoring the predominant position of the Communist Party.

An old man in charge. Brezhnev in East Berlin, 1979, during the Thirtieth Anniversary Celebrations of the German Democratic Republic. Exhausted from speaking, he is being assisted from the speaker's rostrum by East German President Erich Honecker (left) and an aide.

Nuclear Non-proliferation Treaty: Britain, USA and USSR agreed not to transfer their nuclear technology to other nations. France and China did not sign.

Détente

American involvement in Vietnam after 1964 cooled the post-1963 thaw, although the USSR avoided any direct confrontation with the USA. Apart from the 1968 Nuclear Non-proliferation Treaty there was no follow-up to the 1963 Test Ban Treaty. The arms race went on. By 1970 both super-powers had enough intercontinental ballistic missiles (ICBMs) to destroy the world many times over. The quarrel with China worsened, especially during the period of the Cultural Revolution 1966-70. In 1969 serious fighting with many casualties took place along the Amur and Ussuri Rivers on the Russo-Chinese border.

In April 1971 the Russians (and everyone else) were taken by surprise when China made overtures of friendship towards the United States. Alarmed that they might be ganging up against the USSR, Brezhnev took the lead in opening a new and warmer phase in Soviet-American relations, which was called détente and lasted until the late 1970s. The two super-powers agreed to reduce tension in small, practical ways and not to let ideological differences

Full-scale US intervention in Vietnam lasted from 1964 to 1973.

Nixon visited Moscow in May 1972 and 1974. Brezhnev visited Washington DC in 1973.

The space link-up between the crews of an American Apollo and a Soviet Soyuz craft took place on 17 July 1975.

ICBMs are long-range missiles, based either on land or in submarines, which home in directly on their target. They are the main part of the strategic nuclear force, designed to knock an opponent out by totally destroying his main cities. The other type are short and medium-range tactical weapons like the American Cruise and Pershing or the Soviet SS 20, designed to destroy the enemy armed forces. These are the kind of missiles that are based by the USA in Western Europe and the USSR in Eastern Europe and near the Chinese border.

upset world peace. The Vietnam War, which was still going on, was not allowed to stand in the way. Visits were exchanged and a joint space programme planned for 1975. Plans were made for scientific, technological and environmental cooperation and for more student exchanges. A treaty was signed defining the status of Berlin, which ceased to be a world hot spot. The 1975 Helsinki Security Conference finalized Europe's post-war borders. The first Strategic Arms Limitation Treaty (SALT I) was signed in 1972. It did not reduce existing armaments but imposed limitations on the construction of ICBMs for the next five years. Further talks – SALT II – continued throughout the 1970s. During the 4th Arab-Israeli War of 1973 (the Yom Kippur War) a possible confrontation between the super-powers was avoided when Nixon and Brezhnev talked on the Hot Line.

Détente. US President Richard Nixon and Soviet Premier Leonid Brezhnev sign the first stage of the SALT arms control treaty in June 1972.

The Spread of Soviet Power

Détente did not mean an end to the rivalry with the United States for power and influence in the world.

Source A
International Institute for Strategic Studies, London.

The USSR had so many large surface ships in 1970 because most were old and out-of-date. Between 1970 and 1975 many obsolete ships were scrapped and replaced by technologically up-to-date ones.

Soviet military power 1970-77

	1970	1975	1977
Aircraft and helicopter carriers	–	3	3
Major surface ships incl. destroyers and cruisers	226	128	211
Number in armed forces	2,956,000	3,225,000	3,555,000
Tanks	35,000	40,000	41,000

Source B

International Institute for Strategic Studies.

Soviet nuclear power 1970-77

	1970	1975	1977
Nuclear missile – carrying submarines	25	141	143
Land-based ICBMs	1300	1618	1703
Short- and medium-range weapons	*c.* 700	*c.* 1000	*c.* 1000
Total defence expenditure as percentage of annual GNP	8.5	10.6	11–13

Source C

From the briefing given to the incoming foreign minister, Eduard Shevardnadze by his predecessor, Andrei Gromyko, June 1985. Private information given to the *Guardian* correspondent in Moscow, Martin Walker, by a Soviet foreign ministry source. Published in *The Waking Giant*, 1987.

Gromyko told Shevardnadze that the USSR's military inferiority in the Fifties and Sixties had been hidden from the world by the occasional costly success such as the Soviet atom bomb or Sputnik.

Eurasian landmass: combined area of Europe and Asia.

Gromyko began by saying that, until the beginning of 1970, his job as foreign minister had been based very largely on bluff. American superiority in strategic weapons had dominated the bulk of his career . . . . This strategic weakness had been cruelly exposed in 1962 during the Cuban missile crisis . . . .

But after 1970, when the Soviet defence industries had finally produced enough hardware to give the country strategic parity with the Americans, Gromyko had been able to take advantage of the favourable circumstances which developed . . . the psychological mood of isolationism and defeatism which gripped the USA in the wake of the defeat in Vietnam had allowed the Soviet Union to extend its influence far beyond the boundaries of the Eurasian landmass.

? ?

1 What do the figures in Sources A and B tell us about Soviet military power between 1970 and 1977? What types of changes have taken place?

2 What two main purposes (hinted at by Gromyko) are the changes in Soviet military capability intended to achieve? How have circumstances helped the Soviet cause?

3 What effects might the developments above have had on (a) Soviet life at home; (b) the United States?

World Power – the Soviet fleet pays a goodwill visit to Havana, Cuba.

Parity: equality.

Revolutions 1970-79:

Ethiopia 1974: Emperor Haile Selassie replaced by Marxist regime of Colonel Haile Mengistu Mariam.
Angola, Mozambique and Guinea 1975: end of Portuguese colonial rule.
Nicaragua 1979: overthrow of pro-American dictatorship of General Somoza by left-wing Sandanistas.

Local wars and civil wars

The Peoples' Republic of the Yemen v The Yemen Arab Republic.
Ethiopia v breakaway province of Eritrea.
Ethiopia v Somalia over Ogaden region.
In Angola, a post-independence struggle for power between the Marxist MPLA and UNITA, which was backed by South Africa.
In Nicaragua after 1979, war between the Sandanistas and the US-backed Contras.
Yom Kippur war of 1973 between Israel and her Arab neighbours.

Anwar el Sadat succeeded Nasser as president of Egypt in 1970. He was assassinated in 1981.

The Iranian revolution brought to power an anti-Western (but especially anti-American) Islamic regime led by the Ayatollah Khomeini. From November 1979 until January 1981 50 Americans were held hostage in the US embassy in Teheran.

Source A
From Carter's speech on US television, which announced the imposition of sanctions against the USSR, January 1980.

Source B
From a statement by President Brezhnev, published in *Pravda*, 12 January 1980.

The arms race, nuclear and conventional, went on, and so too did the super-power rivalry for the hearts and minds of the people of the world. For the first time the USSR achieved nuclear parity with the West. In the mid-1970s a spate of left-wing revolutions in the Third World turned events in the USSR's favour, although Western suspicions that the Russians were behind the upheavals were almost certainly not justified. The mood of defeatism in the USA, mentioned by Gromyko, also continued. Tanks and aircraft went to help Colonel Mengistu's regime in Ethiopia against the breakaway province of Eritrea and in the war with Somalia (1978–81), 11,000 Cuban soldiers, many armed with Soviet weapons such as Kalashnikov rifles, fought alongside the MPLA in Angola after 1975. Arms and economic aid were sent to the anti-American Colonel Khadafi of Libya, to the Sandanista regime in Nicaragua after 1979, to the Republic of South Yemen in its war with its neighbour and to the Arab states in their quarrel against Israel. In exchange the USSR was able to set up naval bases in the Red Sea (Aden and Socotra Island in the Yemen and Mesewa in Ethiopia), Indian Ocean (Seychelles), Mediterranean (Libya and Syria) and the Atlantic (Guinea). Once almost landlocked, she became in the 1970s a major naval power to rival the USA, with surface fleets in the Indian Ocean, South Atlantic and Mediterranean. The balance in the Cold War seemed at last to be shifting in the USSR's favour. In 1976-7 the Western press grew almost hysterical over rumours that Soviet and Cuban involvement in Angola would win them a naval base in the South Atlantic.

Not all went as smoothly, though, as Gromyko implied. Soviet technicians and advisers in Third World nations were often arrogant and interfering and came to be resented as much as the former colonial powers had been. In 1972 President Sadat ordered the 21,000 Russians out of their bases in Egypt. Hopes of benefiting from the anti-American backlash in Iran after the overthrow of the Shah in 1979 were not realized, for the ruling Islamic clergy disliked Russian communism almost as much. By the mid-1980s the civil wars in both Eritrea and Angola were far from won and had brought few gains. It seems that the huge investment of Soviet arms and money was not really paying off.

The War in Afghanistan

Since December 1978 Afghanistan, on the USSR's southern border, had been controlled by a weak Communist government, unpopular with most of its Muslim subjects and in constant danger of being overthrown and replaced by a fundamentalist Islamic regime like that in Iran. On Christmas Eve 1979 100,000 Soviet troops invaded, the first time since 1945 that the USSR had taken over a country outside the Eastern bloc by force. The reasons for the move are still not entirely clear.

The Soviet invasion of Afghanistan is a callous violation of international law and the United Nations Charter . . . and a deliberate attempt to subjugate an independent Islamic people. Pakistan, Iran and other nations in the region are now in peril, and unless the Kremlin's action is effectively challenged, it could endanger the oil supply and the very existence of the Western nations . . . . The world cannot simply stand by and permit the Soviet Union to commit this act with impunity . . . .

The time came when we could not but respond to the request of the government of friendly Afghanistan . . . . To have acted otherwise would have meant to watch passively the origination on our southern borders of a centre of serious danger to the security of the Soviet state . . . . Soviet troops will be withdrawn as soon as the causes that made the Afghan leadership ask for them have disappeared.

Bogged down – the Red Army in Afghanistan.

Source C

Martin Walker, *The Waking Giant,* pp. 105-6.

In Moscow the invasion was planned as a brief incursion to sort out the chaos of a civil war that was threatening her own security . . . Moscow did not envisage the long and costly guerilla war that followed, nor did it see the Afghan venture as a stepping stone to the Indian Ocean or the oil of the Gulf States.

By the end of the 1970s Moscow was alarmed by the growing wave of Islamic fundamentalism that was lapping on its own southern borders and threatening to bring political instability to the area's Muslim population . . . . So events that have been perceived by the West as evidence of Soviet expansionism have been seen in Moscow as defensive precautions.

? ?

1 Why does none of the three sources above give us a completely reliable and fool-proof explanation of the reasons for the invasion of Afghanistan?

2 From what you have learned so far about the USSR in the 1970s, which of the reasons seem most plausible to you? Give reasons for your answer.

3 How are relations between the USSR and the West likely to be affected by events in Afghanistan?

The Red Army brought with it a new puppet Communist government under Babrak Kamal and were soon bogged down in a war against anti-Communist fighters, the Mujahidin. Like the Americans in Vietnam before them, the Russians learned how hard it was to defeat guerillas operating on their own territory. To flush them out, villages were razed and the countryside was devastated by incendiary bombs and napalm. There were countless civilian casualties and over four million people fled as refugees to Pakistan. By 1982 the war was costing about eight million a day. Great harm was done to the Soviet image abroad, although the full truth was kept from the Soviet people themselves and nothing like the American anti-war protest movement of the Sixties ever developed. But it was all in vain. By the mid-1980s the war in Afghanistan was still far from won, and it was becoming more and more clear that perhaps it never could be.

Jimmy Carter (Democrat), President 1976-80.

Ronald Reagan (Republican), President 1980-88. In a speech in 1983 he dubbed the USSR the 'evil empire'.

SDI, which was nicknamed *Stars Wars* by the Western press, involved firing lasers from orbiting space stations, which would stop enemy missiles before they entered the earth's atmosphere. Although the project was still at the drawing-board stage in 1983 and many American scientists doubted that it was even feasible, its mere possibility would upset the nuclear balance in the USA's favour, for they would be able to attack the USSR without fear of retaliation. Even if the Soviet Union were able to develop her own SDI, this would require an enormous economic investment.

Brezhnev's Politburo – government by old men and the military.

The Death of Détente

Since the mid-1970s détente had been under increasing strain and Afghanistan finished it off. President Carter of the USA cancelled the ratification of SALT II (which had just been signed by the Russians), called off that year's sale of grain and withdrew American athletes from the Moscow Olympics due to be held in July 1980. In November 1980 Ronald Reagan, a sworn enemy of Communism, won the US presidential election. American self-confidence, shattered by events in Vietnam and Iran, revived. The Polish crisis of 1980-81 heightened the tension. The nuclear arms race escalated. By 1983 the Soviet defence budget was rising by over 5 per cent a year, while the economy itself was growing by only about 2-3 per cent.

In the early 1980s, the Americans regained the lead in the arms race. Cruise missiles, which follow the contours of the earth at a distance of 100 feet (30.5m) and could thus avoid an enemy radar screen, were moved into NATO bases in Britain and West Germany. In 1983 Reagan announced his Strategic Defence Initiative or SDI, which, if successful, would make the Soviet nuclear arsenal obsolete overnight. A new Cold War had begun. In the West the blame was laid on the USSR but from Moscow things may have looked very different.

Conclusion

By 1985 the Soviet leadership faced difficult choices. Russian involvement in Africa and Afghanistan was bogged down in a costly stalemate. Relations with the USA were frostier than they had been for a long time, enmeshing the USSR in a new and costlier round of the arms race at a time when her economy was stagnating. From what happened after 1985 it is obvious that the new generation of Soviet leaders had come to believe that it was time for a radical reappraisal of the Soviet goals around the globe.

THE WINDS OF CHANGE
1985~

One of Gorbachev's first breaks with the immediate past was his habit of going on 'walkabouts' and listening to what ordinary people had to say. This had not been seen since Khrushchev's day. Those who knew him in his days as a local party boss recall that even then he was accessible and acted on people's complaints – something relatively rare in Soviet officials.

For Aganbegyan's earlier career, see p. 28.

Oblasts and **Krais**: middle-ranking regional party officials.

Source A
From a speech by Gorbachev to Leningrad party workers in May 1985, shortly after he became Party Secretary.

Introduction

On the death of Chernenko, Mikhail Gorbachev became Party Secretary. At 54, he was the youngest post-war leader, too young to have built his political career under Stalin or to have fought in the Great Patriotic War. Personally, he was approachable, charming and dynamic – a striking contrast with the aged leaders before him – but he inherited a country with many serious problems. The economy was stagnant, the arms race eating up an ever-larger slice of national resources and the war in Afghanistan bogged down in stalemate. Solving these problems might involve asking difficult questions about the very principles on which the Soviet state was founded. Whether any politician who had made his way to the top via the party machines would be able or willing to do this remained doubtful.

Perestroika

Gorbachev first swept away many of the old generation of party apparachiks at all levels. In July 1985 Gromyko was kicked upstairs to the honourable but powerless post of president. 56-year-old Eduard Shevardnadze became foreign minister. The economist, Abel Aganbegyan, was plucked from the political wilderness to become Gorbachev's economic adviser. For the first time in over 40 years, no representative of the armed forces was appointed to the Politburo. Over 40 per cent of the secretaries of *oblasts* and *krais* were replaced between March and December 1985.

This was only the beginning. The USSR would not be a superpower much longer, Gorbachev told his countrymen, unless all aspects of Soviet life were drastically restructured. He called this *perestroika*. At the same time, *glasnost* or 'openness' must replace the old habit of sweeping problems under the carpet and just pretending that they were not there. The 'old boys' network must give way to the right of ordinary citizens to have a say in the way things were run and to criticize, and even sack, corrupt or incompetent Party officials. A step – perhaps – towards that socialist democracy dreamed of by the founders of the Soviet state.

It is obvious that all of us must restructure ourselves, all of us .... Everyone has to master new methods and attitudes and to understand that there is no other way for us .... Why can't we have a quiet life? ... It's been almost seventy years of effort, so to speak, since the October revolution. It would seem that it's possible to relax. No, Comrades, history isn't giving us the chance, at least not now. And I don't know if it will ... calculations show that we need a minimum of four per cent [in the economic growth rate, which was then

running at only about 2-3 per cent a year] – and really we need more – the question is – what can we do? Cut the rate of growth of the standard of living? . . . We can't go down that road.

Our socialist way of life . . . gives the working man confidence in the morrow . . . it is the only way for us and the world . . . the advance of humanity everywhere towards socialism and communism, though uneven, complex and controversial, is inexorable.

Source B
From Gorbachev's speech to the 27th Party Congress, which opened on February 1986.

? ?

1 From what you already know about life in the USSR over the past 20 years, what sort of changes might Gorbachev have in mind when he talks of *perestroika*?

2 In Source C Gorbachev implies that there are limits to the sort of changes that will be allowed. What are these limits?

3 Why are *perestroika* and *glasnost* inseparable?

Glasnost. Citizens of Moscow demonstrate in support of disarmament prior to the 1987 Washington summit meeting between Presidents Reagan and Gorbachev.

Political and economic reforms were introduced that might change the face of the USSR for ever. In the elections for the Supreme Soviet, scheduled for the spring of 1989, more than one candidate, including non-Party members, was able to stand in each constituency. For the first time since 1917 voters might have a genuine choice, although this was not intended to lead to democracy in the Western sense and no rival political parties would be allowed. In May 1988, meetings to form a new party, the Democratic Union, were broken up by the police. Plans were drawn up to dilute the centralized economy with a dose of private enterprise and personal incentives. From the beginning of 1987 two-thirds of Soviet industry was put on a 'self-financing basis'. Factories had to show a profit and could not just write their losses off. Productivity bonuses were to be withheld unless the quality of the goods produced was up to scratch. Collective farmers were to be allowed to sell far more of their produce, especially fruit and vegetables, on the open market. To make up the defects in consumer goods and services, the Co-operative Law came into effect in May 1987, which legalized 29 categories of private, part-time businesses, including taxi-driving, house and car repairs, tailoring and public catering.

A Changing Society

The face of Soviet society began to change. By the spring of 1988 over 100 private restaurants had sprung up in Moscow, where previously there had been only 83 public eating places for a population of over eight million. Foreign journalists were struck by the way people suddenly talked openly on the streets about political prisoners and other such subjects which would have been taboo only a few years before. Outspoken programmes appeared for the first time on television, such as a late-night chat show, *To Midnight and After*, which on one occasion interviewed young Soviet punks, and *Twelfth Storey*, a phone-in programme in which officials faced live questions from viewers. Long-banned films like *Repentance*, which dealt with the Stalinist terror, were screened for the first time. Dissidents including Sakharov and Scheransky were released. The 29th Party Congress held in July 1988 was televised, and was remarkable for its outspoken speeches from the floor. When a serious accident took place at the Chernobyl nuclear power station in April 1986, sending a radioactive cloud out over the rest of Europe, the administration first tried to cover up, as usual. In the end, though, they owned up with a frankness that would have been unimaginable only a few years before, and even asked for medical aid from the West. When an earthquake devastated part of Armenia in December 1987, the Western media were allowed in from the beginning. Under Brezhnev, news of such disasters had been kept even from Soviet citizens themselves. In his speech in November 1987, marking the 70th anniversary of the 1917 revolution, Gorbachev himself spoke of the need to fill in the 'black holes' in Soviet history and to reconsider the past with honesty. For the first time the horrors of collectivization and the purges were discussed openly by Soviet historians.

It did not take long, though, to discover that there were no quick or easy solutions to the USSR's problems.

It would be a mistake to take no notice of a certain increase in the resistance of the conservative forces who see perestroika simply as a threat to their selfish interests and objectives. This resistance can be felt not only at management level but also in work collectives.

Every re-adjustment of the economic mechanism begins with a readjustment of thinking, with a rejection of old stereotypes of thought and actions ... there are those who do not actually want to do anything or change anything. There will be no reconciliation with the stance taken by functionaries of that kind. We will simply have to part ways with them. All the more so do we have to part ways with those who hope that everything will settle down and return to the old ways. That will not happen, comrades!

So things are no better for Svetlana? 'Some prices have actually gone up since *perestroika*', she said, 'Though perhaps the choice is better. It's like watching a magician at the circus. You know it's a trick, but you still applaud.'

She didn't seem particularly sad or angry. But for her and millions of women like her, *perestroika* had made little difference so far.

? ?

1 What obstacles to the success of *perestroika* and *glasnost* is Gorbachev hinting at in Sources A and B? What sorts of people might react in this way and why?

2 What is the potential problem hinted at in Source C?

3 For what other reasons might ordinary Russians become disillusioned with Gorbachev? What effect would this have on his reform programme?

A campaign, similar to those in the West, began to warn Russians about the dangers of AIDS. Such frankness about public health matters would have been unthinkable before 1985.

For the changes in Soviet television since glasnost, see the article entitled *Seeing Red* by Martin Walker in *The Listener*, 7 April, 1988.

Other results of the decline in censorship were the Moscow Art exhibition of January 1987, which allowed artists who had been banned for years to show their paintings; the production of two plays, *The Brest Peace* and *1927*, which featured historical characters like Trotsky, Kamenev and Zinoviev, whose names had not been mentioned officially for years; the publication of *Requiem*, Anna Akhmatova's poem about the mothers of Stalin's victims; and of *Children of the Arbat*, a novel about the families of Stalin's victims in the 1930s, which sold out within hours of its appearing in Soviet bookshops in the winter of 1987.

Source A
From a speech by Mikhail Gorbachev on 2 November 1987, marking the 70th anniversary of the 1917 revolution.

Source B
From a speech by Gorbachev to the Leningrad party workers during a visit to the city in May 1986.

Source C
From an interview with Svetlana Kolatzova, a Moscow librarian and mother, in *The Mail on Sunday*, 4 September 1988.

A new kind of leader. President Gorbachev and his wife Raisa visit the stricken city of Kirovokan following the devastating earthquake which struck Soviet Armenia in December 1987.

Opposition to *perestroika* soon came from people, inside and outside the Party, who had made a good living during the Brezhnev years, and from old-fashioned Party members to whom free discussion and private enterprise were a breach of Communist principles. Conservatives high up in the Party won a significant victory in November 1987, when they forced Gorbachev to sack the Moscow party chief, Boris Yeltsin, an outspoken advocate of a faster pace of reform. Then in October 1988 Gorbachev struck back, when he sacked several of his leading opponents, including his deputy, Yegor Ligachev, and President Gromyko. He took over the presidency himself. So far he seems to be maintaining his powerful position but the future is far from certain.

A more serious obstacle today, however, may be a decline in the public enthusiasm that Gorbachev needs if he is to make *perestroika* work, unless

Mikhail Gorbachev, champion of Glasnost and Perestroika, (right) makes a point to Yegor Ligachev, Politburo conservative (left). Alexander Yakolev, Secretary to the Party Central Committee, plays referee.

Technical triumph: the Soviet space station 'Mir'.

Technical disaster: cleaning up after the Chernobyl catastrophe.

there is a dramatic improvement soon in living standards. So far there is no sign of that and, if anything, things are getting worse. The 1988 harvest was disappointing. The new private businesses have impressed foreign journalists but have so far done little to ease the lot of the man in the street. Their prices are too high and there are few of them outside the big cities. They have even given rise to a new kind of crime. In Moscow a Mafia-type gang threatens private co-operatives and their owners with damage unless they pay 'security money'. The rescue operation after the Armenian earthquake was a shambles and seen by the rest of the world to be so. There was next to no co-ordination between the various agencies involved and a shortage of everything from excavators needed to dig survivors out to tents and antibiotics.

The reasons for the failures are complex. It is difficult, as Gorbachev himself has confessed, to change the working habits of generations in a hurry. The new work habits being demanded mean immediate sacrifices and only long-term rewards, which may never come. For many ordinary Russians, for example, the first impact of the quality-control campaign has been a drop in wages, sometimes by as much as 30 per cent. On the farm, the incentive to work hard is still not strong enough. An attempt was made to solve this in the spring of 1989 by the introduction of sweeping reforms, including a law allowing farmers to lease land for their own use and sell the produce on the open market. Whether this will lead to a quick end to food shortages remains to be seen. The danger that, still struggling with daily queues, people will just lose interest in *perestroika* is still very real. When Gorbachev visited the Siberian city of Krasnoyorsk in September 1988, he was mobbed in the streets by angry citizens complaining about housing and food shortages. In the summer of 1989 the economy was almost brought to a standstill when miners in Siberia and the Ukraine went on strike. The Soviet people's faith in Mr Gorbachev was evaporating fast.

Glasnost and relaxation of the police state is already having unforeseen consequences that threaten the very fabric of the USSR itself. Early in 1988 an old quarrel between the southern republics of Armenia and Azerbaijan over the tiny territory of Nagorny Karabakh flared up into outright racial violence. In the town of Sumgait, where 200 people died in rioting in February that year, the army had to be sent in to calm things down. Thousands of Armenians living in Azerbaijan fled from their homes in fear of their lives. The tension rumbled on throughout the year and was no nearer a solution at the end. In the Baltic Republics huge popular demonstrations have taken place for greater economic and cultural freedom and even for outright independence. So far a show-down has been avoided but the implications for the future are ominous, especially if the nationalist movement should spread to other areas like Georgia or the Ukraine. If President Gorbachev gives in, the USSR will cease to exist in its present form. If he clamps down, especially by force, it will mean the end of *perestroika* and perhaps of Gorbachev's own career, for the conservatives will then be able to say, 'I told you so'.

Many local party officials tried to manipulate the March 1989 elections to bring about the result that they wanted. Just like in the old days, there were many constituencies where a single Communist Party candidate stood unopposed. The results, though, were far from following the old pattern. Wherever reformers stood, they ran away with the votes. The most spectacular examples were Boris Yeltsin, who won 90 per cent of the Moscow votes, and the Leningrad Party chief, who was routed five to one by an unknown shipyard worker. Where only one person stood, electors often expressed their dissatisfaction by crossing out the name on their ballot paper and making sure that the candidate did not get the 50 per cent of the vote he needed to be elected. The Party boss and the mayor of Kiev (the USSR's third largest city) both lost in this way. In the Baltic States nationalists swept the

Rupert Cornwell in *The Independent*, 28 March 1989.

At Reykjavik Gorbachev offered to accept President Reagan's idea for a 'zero option' deal, which would remove medium-range weapons including Cruise missiles from Europe, and laid down a plan of his own for 50 per cent cuts on both US and Soviet strategic arsenals, with a commitment to their total abolition by the year 2000 – far more sweeping cuts than either side had ever proposed before.

Source A
From President Gorbachev's speech to the United Nations General Assembly, 7 December 1988.

board. It was, wrote one Western journalist the next day, 'the most astonishing rebuke the country's entrenched Communist apparatus has had in the 70 years it had run the country'. What would happen next no one knew. It might be the start of the road to multi-party democracy or it might trigger the conservatives off into fighting back again.

The New Thaw

The reforms at home were more than matched by the sweeping changes Gorbachev brought about in Soviet foreign policy and its relations with the USA. Gorbachev and Reagan met in Geneva in November 1985 and Reykjavik (Iceland) in October 1986, when far-reaching arms control proposals made by the Soviet leader foundered on Gorbachev's insistence that the USA abandon SKI (the Strategic Defence Initiative) and Reagan's refusal to do so. Contacts continued, however, and in December 1987 Gorbachev visited Washington and signed the Intermediate Nuclear Forces (INF) Treaty, which abolished many of the short-range nuclear weapons both sides kept in Europe. For the first time foreign observers were allowed on Soviet soil to verify whether her side of the treaty was being kept. In the summer of 1988 the world saw the surprising sight of top Soviet and American army officers touring each others' military bases. Talks were begun on a Strategic Arms Reduction Treaty (START) to cut arsenals of long-range, intercontinental missiles by 50 per cent; they have not yet come to a conclusion. Another summit meeting was held in Moscow in May 1988. Gorbachev himself became something of a media star in the West and did much to transform the USSR's image abroad.

All this, though, was but a lead-up to the astounding events of 1988. In April 1988 the USSR announced that over the next 10 months it would withdraw most of its troops from Afghanistan, which Gorbachev had publicly called a 'bleeding wound'. They kept their word. On 15 February 1989 the last Soviet soldier came home. To the Soviet public it was depicted as an honourable withdrawal at the end of a successful campaign but in reality the Russians were abandoning President Najibullah and the Afghan Communists to their fate. It was the first real breach in the Brezhnev Doctrine. A cease-fire was signed in Angola in September 1988. Talks to establish better relations were opened with the Chinese. The highlight came, though, at the United Nations in December 1988, when Gorbachev, appearing there in person, made a speech that shook the world – a speech no one had ever expected to hear from a Soviet leader. Delegates from 159 nations stood up to applaud him as he finished. Among his proposals was an offer to take the first step towards disarmament by cutting Soviet armed forces by 10 per cent, including 50,000 troops, 10,000 tanks and 80 aircraft now stationed in Eastern Europe, and nearly all those on the Chinese frontier. This, he hoped, would inspire the West to do the same and be only the start of a much bigger disarmament.

We are witnessing the most profound social change .... Some past differences and disputes are losing their importance, but conflicts of a different kind are taking their place. Life is making us abandon established stereotypes and outdated views ... it would be a mistake to think that the problems plaguing mankind today can be solved with means and methods which were applied or seemed to work in the past ... today we face a different world for which we must seek a different road to the future ... it is obvious, for example, that the use or threat of force can no longer and must no longer be an instrument of foreign policy. This applies, above all, to nuclear arms. But that is not the only thing that matters. All of us, and primarily the stronger of us, must exercise self-restraint and totally rule out any use of force.

Source B
From an article by Peter Jenkins in
The Independent, 21 December 1988.

Source C
The Daily Telegraph, 9 December 1988.

circumspection: great caution.

Occasionally a year goes down in history as the end or beginning of an era
. . . . It may well be that 1988 will go down as an *annus mirabilis*, the year of
Gorbachev, of momentous events in the Soviet Union and the Communist
world, the year in which the old post-war order began to give way to the new,
the beginning of the end of the Cold War.

The Soviet leader cannot complain if we unwrap his gift with circumspection.
We have lived through too many cheerless winters in East-West relations
since the war to be enthused by wrapping alone . . . . Since the Soviet Union
enjoys a huge preponderance in many classes of weaponry, Mr Gorbachev can
afford to be generous and there is always the fear that what has been taken
away can swiftly be replaced . . . . And even the motives for his speech are not
beyond suspicion, for we can guess that one reason for the offer to reduce
Soviet tanks and weaponry is the desperate need to convert some of the Soviet
defence factories to serve the hard-pressed consumer industries . . . . This is
not to underrate the importance of Mr Gorbachev's speech yesterday. But gift
horses must expect to be greeted cautiously when they have bitten so often.

? ?

1 What 'profound' changes do you think Gorbachev has in mind in Source A?
How does he think they have altered world politics for ever? Does this speech
throw light on everything Gorbachev has been doing since 1985?

2 What does Peter Jenkins think is the significance of these events?

3 In what ways and why is the *Daily Telegraph* editorial more cautious than the
writer of Source B?

*New face. Ronald Reagan introduces US
President elect George Bush to President
Gorbachev, December 1988.*

Glasnost in action. A scene from Alexander Getman's stage version of A Tortuous Path *by Ye. Ginzburg, which deals with the labour camps of the Stalinist period.*

The dramatic changes in Eastern Europe in 1989 have convinced most observers in the West that Gorbachev's foreign policies mark a complete break with the past – in particular, his refusal to intervene in the internal politics of Poland, Czechoslovakia or Romania. Whether Gorbachev can hold on to power in the face of increasing nationalist pressure from within the Soviet Republics remains to be seen.

It is too early to judge for certain whether the USSR is calling a real end to the Cold War. Many Westerners are still suspicious, fearing that Soviet aims have not really changed and that Gorbachev is merely buying himself a breathing space or that he may soon be replaced at home by a Communist hardliner of the old school. Others, who believe he is genuinely a man of peace, fear that his vision may die because the West is too distrustful and stuck in old ways of thinking to take it up. Only time will tell.

Conclusion

Over the past three years Soviet life has been subjected to a wave of self-criticism that has not been seen since the early days of the state. It is easy to find fault, as many in the West have done, and to ignore just how difficult it is to transform a society overnight and just how much *has* changed since 1985. *Perestroika*, though, is under increasing threat inside the USSR itself – especially from nationalist tensions and from its failure to bring any noticeable improvement to the daily lives of most Soviet citizens. How it will go in the future is anyone's guess. Progress towards a freer and more democratic society may continue or the experiment may falter and die. Restless republics like Latvia or Estonia may be allowed to go their own way, changing the shape of the USSR for good, or held in by force, as in Stalin's day. The events of 1988 may mean an end to the Cold War or just another short-lived thaw. The fate of the USSR and its 230 million people is poised on a knife-edge.

USSR

YEAR BY YEAR

SINCE 1945

1945 Yalta Conference.
Surrender of Germany.
Potsdam Conference and division of
Germany.
Rigged elections in Hungary bring
Communist Party to power.
Re-annexation of Baltic States.

1946 4th Five-Year plan.
Decree ordering re-establishment of
collective farms.
Famine in Ukraine.
Zhdanovshchina (purge) begins.
Akhmatova expelled from
Writers' Union.
Churchill's Iron Curtain speech.

1947 Establishment of COMINFORM.

1948 Lysenko's biological theories
become official policy.
Death of Zhdanov.
Leningrad Affair.
Communist take-over of
Czechoslovakia.
Expulsion of Yugoslavia from
COMINFORM.
Berlin Blockade begun.

1949 Molotov sacked as Foreign
Minister; his wife sent to camp.
First Soviet atomic bomb successfully
tested.
Berlin Blockade called off.
Foundation of COMECON.
Foundation of German Democratic
Republic (East Germany).

1950 Industrial output passes pre-war
level.
Korean War begins.
Treaty of Friendship and Mutual
Assistance with China.

1951 5th Five-Year Plan.

1952 Czechoslovak purge.

1953 *Pravda* uncovers 'Doctors' Plot.
Death of Stalin.
Execution of Beria.
Collective leadership of Malenkov and
Khrushchev.
Public acknowledgement of the failure
of Soviet Agriculture.
First Soviet hydrogen bomb.
Ceasefire in Korea.
East Berlin uprising.

1954 Virgin Lands scheme begins.
Publication of *The Thaw* and *Not by
Bread Alone.*
Geneva Conference on Indo-China.

1955 Bulganin replaces Malenkov as
Prime Minister.
Warsaw Pact formed.
Reconciliation with Yugoslavia.
Geneva Summit Conference.
Peace treaty with Austria.

1956 20th Party conference and
Khrushchev's 'secret speech'.
End of Stalin's labour laws.
Visit of Bulganin and Khrushchev to
Britain.
Disturbances in Poland; Gomulka
becomes Party Secretary.
Hungarian uprising and Soviet invasion.

1957 Khrushchev defeats attempt to
overthrow him: Molotov sacked.
Pasternak's *Dr Zhivago* published in
Italy.
Gromyko becomes Foreign Minister.
Decentralization of industrial planning.
Sputnik launched.

1958 Khrushchev becomes Prime
Minister.
Pasternak awarded Nobel prize for
literature.

1959 Seven-Year Plan announced.

Maize campaign.
Khrushchev's visit to the USA.

1960 U2 incident and collapse of
Paris Summit.
Quarrel with China.

1961 22nd Party Congress and
further denunciation of Stalin; his
body removed from mausoleum.
7th Five-Year Plan.
Gagarin becomes first man in space.
Erection of Berlin Wall.

1962 Publication of *One Day in the
Life of Ivan Denisovitch.*
Yevtushenko's poem *Stalin's Heirs*
published in *Pravda.*
Cuban Missile Crisis.

1963 Official warnings that
destalinization and artistic
freedom have gone far enough.
Poor harvest and purchase of grain from
USA.
Hot Line set up.
Partial Nuclear Test Ban Treaty.

1964 Khrushchev's downfall;
Brezhnev becomes Party
Secretary.

1966 Trial of Sinyavsky and Daniel.
Defection of Stalin's daughter,
Svetlana.

1968 First issue of *Journal of Current
Events.*
Soviet invasion of Czechoslovakia;
Brezhnev Doctrine.

1969 Publication of *A Week Like Any
Other* in *Novy Mir.*

1970 Solzhenitsyn awarded Nobel
prize for literature.

1971 Reconciliation between USA
and China.

1972 Georgian corruption scandal; Shevardnadze appointed as Party leader there.
Nixon's visit to Moscow.
SALT II signed.
Expulsion of Soviet advisers from Egypt.

1973 Yom Kippur War.

1974 Deportation of Solzhenitsyn.

1975 Helsinki conference on human rights and European security.
Angolan civil war begins.

1976 Formation of Helsinki Watch group.

1977 Brezhnev replaces Podgorny as President.
Demonstration in Georgia against use of Russian language there.
Treaty of friendship with Ethiopia.

1978 Imprisonment of Shcharansky.

1979 Invasion of Afghanistan.

1980 Death of Kosygin; Tikhonov becomes Prime Minister.
Exile of Sakharov to Gorky.
Moscow Olympics.
Formation of Solidarity trade union in Poland.

1981 Martial Law declared in Poland.

1982 Death of Brezhnev; Andropov becomes Party Secretary.

1983 Reagan announces SDI.

1984 Death of Andropov; Chernenko's appointment as Party Secretary.

1985 Death of Chernenko; Gorbachev becomes Party Secretary.
Sweeping personnel changes; Shevardnadze replaces Gromyko as Foreign Minister.
Geneva Summit.

1986 27th Party Conference; Gorbachev outlines *perestroika* and *glasnost*.
Chernobyl nuclear disaster.
Serious riots in Kazakhstan.
Release of Sakharov.
Reykjavik Summit.

1987 Co-operative Law passed.
Dismissal of Yeltsin as Moscow Party chief.
Washington Summit; INF treaty signed.

1988 Outspoken 29th Party Congress.
Rioting in Armenia and Azerbaijan over border dispute.
Moscow Summit.
Withdrawal from Afghanistan begins.
Ceasefire in Angola.

1989 First elections to Supreme Soviet under new electoral law.
Last Soviet troops leave Afghanistan.
Siberian miners strikes.

BOOK LIST

Books on the History of the USSR 1945 to the Present Day
R.W. Davies (ed.) *The Soviet Union*, Allen and Unwin 1978
M. Franklin, *Khrushchev*, Penguin, 1968
G. Hosking, *A History of the Soviet Union*, Fontana, 1985
P.J. Larkin, *World History in the 20th Century: USA and Russia*, Hulton Educational, 1968
M. McCauley, *The Soviet Union since 1917*, Longman, 1981
A. Nove, *An Economic History of the USSR*, Pelican, 1978
M. Walker, *The Waking Giant. The Soviet Union under Gorbachev*, Sphere Books, 1988
A. Werth, *Russia, The Post-War Years*, Robert Hale and Co., 1971

Books on Soviet Life
M. Binyon, *Life in Russia*, Heinemann, 1983
A. Bookbinder, O. Lichtenstein and R. Denton, *Comrades*, BBC Publications 1985
H. Salisbury (ed.), *Anatomy of the Soviet Union*, New York Times Books, 1967. A portrait of the USSR in the mid-1960s.
H. Smith, *The Russians*, Times Books, 1976

Memoirs
S. Alliluyeva, *Twenty Letters to a Friend*, Penguin, 1968
S. Alliluyeva, *Only One Year*, Penguin, 1971

A. Almarik, *Involuntary Journey to Siberia*, Alfred Knopf, 1982
M. Djilas, *Conversations with Stalin*, Pelican, 1963
N. Khrushchev, *Khrushchev Remembers*, Sphere Books, 1971
A. Solzhenitsyn, *The Gulag Archipelago*, 3 vols, Fontana, 1974, 1975, 1978

Works of Fiction available in English
R. Milner-Gulland and P. Levin (ed.), *Yevtushenko, Selected Poems*, Penguin, 1962
A. Solzhenitsyn, *Cancer Ward*, Penguin, 1968
A. Solzhenitsyn, *One Day in the Life of Ivan Denisovitch*, Gollancz, 1963
A. Solzhenitsyn, *The First Circle*, Fontana, 1970

SKETCHES OF IMPORTANT FIGURES

Alliluyeva, Svetlana, (1926-)
Stalin's daughter (Alliluyeva was her mother's maiden name), who defected to the West in 1966 and published there two volumes of memoirs, *Twenty Letters to a Friend* (written in secret in 1963) and *Only One Year* (1969). These give an inside, if very personal, view of life at the top in Stalin's Russia.

Almarik, Andrei (1938-80)   Russian historian who first clashed with the authorities in 1960 when he refused to change his doctoral thesis to make it more politically acceptable. Exiled to Siberia in 1965, on his release he wrote *Will the Soviet Union Survive until 1984?* and *Involuntary Journey to Siberia*, both of which were published in the West and earned him a further spell in a labour camp 1970-76. In 1976, he was given permission to emigrate to the West and died in a car crash in Spain in 1980.

Andropov, Yuri (1914-84)   Party official, who began his career as a Komsomol organizer. During the war he helped organize partisan detachments behind German lines. Soviet ambassador to Hungary at time of 1956 uprising. Head of KGB 1967-82. Became Party Secretary on death of Brezhnev in November 1982 but fell seriously ill soon after. Died in February 1984.

Beria, Lavrenty P. (1899-1953)
Georgian, who became head of the NKVD in 1938, after the previous chief, Yezhov, was purged. Between 1938 and 1953, he was one of the most feared men in the USSR, even among his Party colleagues, who ganged up on him after Stalin's death and had him executed.

Brezhnev, Leonid I. (1906-82)   A Communist Party official, who rose to the top under the patronage of Khrushchev. Politburo member from 1957 and Khrushchev's successor as Party Secretary in 1964, after having probably taken part in the plot to overthrow him. Leader of the USSR until his death in 1982 and President from 1977. A proponent of détente abroad, but an opponent of change and liberalization at home, his years in power are generally regarded as a time of economic and political stagnation, when crucial social problems were swept under the carpet.

Chernenko, Konstantin (1911-85)
Son of a Siberian peasant, who worked with Brezhnev during the war and rose to the top under his influence as one of the Dnieper Mafia. Appointed as stop-gap Party Secretary in February 1984 (the oldest man ever to be chosen for the post), he died the following March without having made any impact.

Gorbachev, Mikhail S. (1931-)
Son of a peasant from the Stavropol region of Southern Russia, who became a professional Party worker after graduating from Moscow University in 1955. Moved up the Party hierarchy under the patronage of Kulakov to become a member of the Politburo in 1980 and Party Secretary in March 1985. Architect of campaigns for revitalization and democratization of Soviet life, called in Russian *perestroika* and *glasnost*, and for an end to the nuclear arms race.

Gromyko, Andrei (1909-1989)
Professional diplomat who served as foreign minister from 1957-85. President of the USSR from 1985.

Khrushchev, Nikita (1896-1971)
Son of a peasant and metal-worker by trade, Khrushchev rose to the top as a result of the purges of the 1930s, becoming Ukrainian party boss 1938-49 and a member of the Politburo from 1939. Appointed Party Secretary in the collective leadership after Stalin's death, he had made himself sole ruler of the USSR by 1957, until he was sacked by his Politburo colleagues in October 1964. Instigator of the destalinization campaign and leader of USSR during Cuban crisis. For his career 1957-64, see chapter 5. Spent the last seven years of his life in retirement and died in obscurity. In 1971 his memoirs – the first ever written by a Soviet leader – were published in the West and have become an invaluable source for historians on the last years of Stalin.

Lenin, Vladimir I. (1870-1924)
Born Vladimir Ulyanov, he was the founder and leader of the Russian Bolshevik (later renamed Communist) Party 1903-17, and first leader of the Soviet state from 1917 until his death in 1924. Revered still as the father of the Soviet Union, his own version of Marxism (altered to fit it in with Russian conditions) called Marxism-Leninism is the official ideology of the USSR.

Malenkov, Georgy M. (1902-88)
Communist Party official, who rose to the top during the purges of the 1930s. Widely tipped as Stalin's most likely successor. Shared power with Khrushchev after 1953 and was the first of the new Soviet leaders to put the case for consumer goods. Outmanoeuvred by Khrushchev and ousted from the prime ministership in 1955. Denounced in the 'secret speech' as the man most responsible after Stalin for the post-1945 purges and sent to manage a power station in Soviet Central Asia. Lived out the rest of his life in obscurity.

Molotov, Vyacheslav M. (1890-1985)
Born Vyacheslav M. Scriabin, he became a Communist in 1906 and was a close associate of Stalin. Foreign Minister of the USSR 1939-49 and 1953-7, and played a prominent role in the 1939 Pact with Germany (often called the Molotov-Ribbentrop Pact) and in the development of the Cold War and the Soviet empire in Eastern Europe after 1945. At odds with Khrushchev over destalinization and reconciliation with Yugoslavia, he was sacked in 1957 and lived the rest of his life in obscurity.

Sakharov, Andrei (1921-   )
Nuclear physicist who played a key role in the construction of the first Soviet hydrogen bomb in 1953. In the late 1950s his growing awareness of the damage done by radiation turned him against nuclear research, and his frustration at his inability to talk about these issues in public turned him into a campaigner for human rights, scientific freedom and an end to the arms race and into conflict with the Soviet authorities. Winner of Nobel peace prize 1975. Exiled with his wife to the town of Gorky in 1980 and released in 1986. Elected to Supreme Soviet in March 1989 and became a forthright critic of the shortcomings of perestroika.

Shevardnadze, Eduard (1928-   )
Georgian party worker, who was sent to investigate the corruption scandals there in 1972. Appointed as Foreign Minister of the USSR in July 1985.

Solzhenitsyn, Alexander (1918-   )
Russian writer who spent the years 1945-53 in labour camps for criticizing Stalin in a private letter. His short story about life in the camps, *One Day in the Life of Ivan Denisovitch*, was published in 1962 in the USSR, during the short-lived thaw of 1961-2 and was a great sensation. During the clamp-down on free expression after 1963, his criticisms of the Soviet system past and present made him increasingly a marked man with the authorities and he was forcibly expelled from the USSR in 1974. He settled in the USA, where he published *The Gulag Archipelago*, an in-depth account of the Stalinist labour camps taken from the testimonies of prisoners. Winner of 1970 Nobel prize for literature.

Stalin, Josef V. (1879-1953)   Born Josef. V. Djugashvili in Georgia, he joined the Bolshevik party in 1904 and took part in the 1917 revolution and civil war that followed, although his role was always eclipsed by more flamboyant personalities like Trotsky. Appointed General Secretary of the Communist Party in 1922, he used the post to outmanoeuvre his rivals, including Trotsky, and to make himself dictator of the USSR until his death. For his career between 1927 and 1953, see chapters 1-3. Partially discredited after his death in the destalinization campaign.

Tvardovsky, Alexander T. (1910-71)
Poet, who was editor of the literary magazine *Novy Mir* 1950-54 and 1958-70, when it published articles and stories uncovering some of the truth about life in Stalin's Russia, including *Not by Bread Alone* and *One Day in the Life of Ivan Denisovitch*. Sacked in 1970 during the Brezhnev clampdown on artistic freedom.

Yevtushenko, Yevgeny A. (1933-   )
Russian poet, who first attracted public attention during the thaw after Stalin's death with his long poem *Zima Railway Station*, which describes the confusion of the young in post-Stalinist Russia, and became a symbol of the struggle of writers for freer expression and the right to expose the crimes of the past. Among his best-known works are *Stalin's Heirs* and *Babi Yar* (1962).

Zhdanov, Andrei A. (1896-1948)
Close associate of Stalin, who became Leningrad Party leader in 1934 and played a key role in defending the city during the German siege October 1941 to January 1944. In charge of cultural affairs 1945-8 and responsible for the purge of non-orthodox artists and scientists known as the Zhdanovchina. Died in 1948, apparently of natural causes.

INDEX

The figures in **bold type** refer to the pages on which illustrations appear